BROADEN YOUR VOCABULARY

Apply Simple Greek and Latin Roots To Learn Hundreds of New English Words

Spencer Donahoe

Historical Audiobooks

Copyright © 2024 Spencer Donahoe

All rights reserved

The characters and events portrayed in this book are fictitious. Any similarity to real persons, living or dead, is coincidental and not intended by the author.

No part of this book may be reproduced, or stored in a retrieval system, or transmitted in any form or by any means, electronic, mechanical, photocopying, recording, or otherwise, without express written permission of the publisher.

CONTENTS

Title Page
Copyright
Introduction
Understanding Common Affixes (Prefixes and Suffixes)   2
Root: "aqua-" (Meaning: "water")   6
Root: "-tere-" (Meaning: "earth" or "land")   8
Root: "vid-" or "vis-" (Meaning: "see" or "look")   11
Root: "phobia" (Meaning: "fear")   14
Root: "tract-" (Meaning: "Pull" or "Drag")   16
Root: "morph" (Meaning: "form" or "shape")   19
Root: "scrib-" or "script-" (Meaning: "write")   21
Root: "techno" (Meaning: "art" or "skill")   24
Root: "voc-" or "vok-" (Meaning: "call" or "voice")   28
Root: "path-" (Meaning: "feeling" or "suffering")   31
Root: "auto-" (Meaning: "self")   34
Root: - "tele-" (Meaning: "far" or "distant")   36
Root: "therm-" (Meaning: "heat")   40
Root: "port-" (Meaning: "Carry")   43
Root: "sub-" (Meaning: "under" or "below")   46
Root: "aud-" (Meaning: "hear" or "listen")   49

Root	Page
Root: "phil-" (Meaning: "love" or "affinity for")	52
Root: "geo-" (Meaning: "earth" or "ground")	56
Root: "bio-" (Meaning: "life")	60
Root: "phon-" (Meaning: "sound" or "voice")	63
Root: "dict-" (Meaning: "speak" or "say")	66
Root: "ject-" (Meaning: "throw")	69
Root: "viv-" (Meaning: "life")	72
Root: "duc-" (Meaning: "lead")	75
Root: "spect-" (Meaning: "look" or "see")	78
Root: - "vert-" (Meaning: "turn")	81
Root: "form-" (Meaning: "shape" or "form")	84
Root: "vers-" (Meaning: "turn")	87
Root: "grad-" (Meaning: "step" or "degree")	90
Root: "cred-" (Meaning: "believe" or "trust")	93
Root: "mit-" or "miss-" (Meaning: "send")	96
Root: "cide-" (Meaning: "kill" or "cut")	98
Root: "circum-" (Meaning: "around")	101
Root: "tempor-" (Meaning: "time")	104
Root: "agn-" (Meaning: "To Know" or "Recognize")	107
Root: "jur-" (Meaning: "Law" or "Right")	110
Root: "clam-" (Meaning: "Shout" or "Cry Out")	113
Root: "poly-" (Meaning: "Many")	116
Root: "sent-" (Meaning: "Feel" or "Think")	119
Root: "fract-" (Meaning: "Break")	122
Root: "gen-" (Meaning: "Birth" or "Race")	125
Root: "pan-" (Meaning: "All" or "Every")	128
Root: "pater-" (Meaning: "Father")	131
Root: "pel-" (Meaning: "Drive" or "Push")	134

Root	Page
Root: "soci-" (Meaning: "Companion" or "Society")	137
Root: "pend-" (Meaning: "Hang" or "Weigh")	140
Root: "log-" (Meaning: "Word" or "Study")	143
Root: "act-" (Meaning: "Do" or "Drive")	146
Root: "man-" (Meaning: "Hand")	149
Root: "sect-" (Meaning: "Cut" or "Separate")	154
Root: "reg-" (Meaning: "Rule" or "Direct")	157
Root: "fug-" (Meaning: "Flee" or "Run")	160
Root: "vol-" (Meaning: "Wish" or "Will")	163
Root: "vi-" (Meaning: "Life")	166
Root: "frig-" (Meaning: "Cold")	169
Root: "fid-" (Meaning: "Faith" or "Trust")	172
Root: "dyna-" (Meaning: "Power")	176
Root: "ver-" (Meaning: "True")	179
Root: "luc-" (Meaning: "Light")	182
Root: "cent-" (Meaning: "Hundred")	185
Root: "dox-" (Meaning: "Opinion" or "Belief")	188
Root: "agri-" (Meaning: "Field" or "Farm")	192
Root: "sol-" (Meaning: "Alone" or "Sun")	196
Root: "virt-" (Meaning: "Strength" or "Power")	199
Root: "lun-" (Meaning: "Moon")	203
Root: "chrono-" (Meaning: "Time")	207
Root: "volv-" (Meaning: "Roll" or "Turn")	210
Root: "inter-" (Meaning: "Between" or "Among")	213
Root: "aster-" (Meaning: "Star")	216
Root: "anim-" (Meaning: "Life" or "Spirit")	220
Root: "tact-" (Meaning: "Touch")	224
Root: "bibl-" (Meaning: "Book")	227

Root: "plac-" (Meaning: "Please" or "Calm")	230
Root: "pol-" (Meaning: "City" or "Community")	233
Root: "flor-" (Meaning: "Flower")	237
Root: "lith-" (Meaning: "Stone" or "Rock")	240
Root: "chrom-" (Meaning: "Color")	244
Root: "eco-" (Meaning: "House" or "Environment")	247
Root: "orth-" (Meaning: "Straight" or "Correct")	251
Root: "carn-" (Meaning: "Flesh" or "Meat")	254
Root: "pneu-" (Meaning: "Breath" or "Lung")	256
Root: "mater-" (Meaning: "Mother")	258
Root: "uni-" (Meaning: "One")	261
Root: "fer-" (Meaning: "Carry" or "Bring")	264
Root: "anthrop-" (Meaning: "Human")	267
Root: "ped-" (Meaning: "Foot")	270
Root: "hydra-" (Meaning: "Water")	273
Root: "capit-" (Meaning: "Head")	276
Root: "san-" (Meaning: "Health")	279
Root: "rect-" (Meaning: "Straight" or "Right")	282
Root: "mut-" (Meaning: "Change")	285
Root: "mort-" (Meaning: "Death")	288
Root: "mono-" (Meaning: "One" or "Single")	291
Root: "migr-" (Meaning: "Move")	295
Root: "lev-" (Meaning: "Light" or "Lift")	298
Root: "lat-" (Meaning: "Side" or "Wide")	301
Root: "jov-" (Meaning: "Jupiter" or "Good")	304
Root: "ign-" (Meaning: "Fire")	307
Root: "hypo-" (Meaning: "Under" or "Below")	310
Root: "equi-" (Meaning: "Equal")	313

Root: "dur-" (Meaning: "Hard" or "Lasting")   316
Root: "duct-" (Meaning: "Lead" or "Conduct")   319
Root: "dem-" (Meaning: "People")   322
Root: "crypt-" (Meaning: "Hidden")   325
Root: "cre-" (Meaning: "Create" or "Grow")   328
Root: "cor-" (Meaning: "Heart")   331
Root: "clin-" (Meaning: "Lean" or "Slope")   334
Root: "calor-" (Meaning: "Heat")   336
Root: "brev-" (Meaning: "Short")   339

INTRODUCTION

You're about to learn hundreds of new words using a powerful linguistic method. That method is word roots.

So much of our vocabulary today originates from ancient languages that came before English, chiefly Greek and Latin. Often simple short stems from these languages determine a word's meaning. If you learn these stems, it's a force multiplier, you can understand whole range of words from a single stem. This makes focusing on these word stems the single most effective way to broaden your vocabulary.

So let's dive in and use this simple, powerful method to broaden your vocabulary. In addition to explaining these word stems, you'll also see vocabulary presented in multiple ways to help you learn it and spot nuances of usage.

BROADEN YOUR ENGLISH VOCABULARY

Apply Simple Greek and Latin Roots To Learn Hundreds of New English Words

UNDERSTANDING COMMON AFFIXES (PREFIXES AND SUFFIXES)

Affixes are added to root words to change their meanings. They can be categorized into *two main types:*
- **Prefixes:** Added at the <u>beginning of a word,</u> often altering its meaning or turning it into an opposite or related concept.
    - *Example*: **Un**happy, **Re**write, **Pre**historic, **Dis**agree, **Mis**understood
- **Suffixes:** Added at the <u>end of a word,</u> often changing the word's function (e.g., from noun to adjective) or its intensity.
    - *Example:* Joy**ful**, Hope**less**, Read**able**, Quick**ly**, Develop**ment**
    - **Note:** *There are affixes that can appear in the <u>middle of words,</u> and these are known as **Infixes**. However, in English, infixes are rare, but they do exist, often as informal or emphatic additions. (Example: Un-freaking-believable, Abso-bloody-lutely!)*

        *In addition, there are affixes that is added to <u>both the beginning and end of a root word</u> simultaneously, and these are known as **Circumfixes**. Just like Infixes, Circumfixes are not common in English, yet they are* *prominent in other languages, such as German and certain indigenous languages.*

Some affixes carry **positive connotations** (e.g., -ful as in hopeful or care- as in caretaker). Others have **negative connotations** (e.g., -less as in fearless or dis- as in disagree).

Prefix/Suffix	Connotation	Meaning	Example Words	Explanation
in- / im-	Negative	Not, without	inevitable, impolite	In *inevitable*, "in-" means unavoidable; in *impolite*, it denotes rudeness
dis-	Negative	Opposite of, not	disagree, disrespect	"Dis-" shows opposition or negation
-less	Negative	Without	fearless, hopeless	"-less" implies a lack of something
un-	Negative	Not, opposite of	unfair, uncertain	Adds a negative meaning, such as in *unfair*
re-	Neutral	Again, back	rewrite, rebuild	Indicates repetition
-ful	Positive	Full of	hopeful, joyful	Adds a positive meaning, suggesting abundance
-er / -or	Positive/Neutral	One who does	caretaker, actor	Refers to a person doing the action
-able / -ible	Positive	Capable of	adaptable, visible	Indicates possibility or capability

Exercise 1: List Additional Words with the Same Affixes
1. **Words with "in- / im-" (Negative):**
    - *Inaccurate*: Not accurate
    - *Immovable*: Unable to be moved
    - *Inappropriate*: Not appropriate
2. **Words with "dis-" (Negative):**
    - *Disloyal*: Not loyal
    - *Disagreeable*: Unpleasant or hard to get along with
    - *Disapprove*: To not approve or accept
3. **Words with "-less" (Negative):**
    - *Helpless*: Without help
    - *Careless*: Without care or caution
    - *Hopeless*: Without hope
4. **Words with "-ful" (Positive):**
    - *Joyful*: Full of joy

- *Respectful*: Showing respect
- *Powerful*: Full of power or strength

Exercise 2: Changing Affixes to Modify Meaning

Given a root word, add prefixes or suffixes to create new words. Note the shift in meaning with each change.

1. **Root**: *Hope*
   - *Hopeful* (positive connotation, showing optimism)
   - *Hopeless* (negative connotation, showing despair)
2. **Root**: *Respect*
   - *Respectful* (positive connotation, showing regard)
   - *Disrespect* (negative connotation, showing lack of regard)
3. **Root**: *Agree*
   - *Agreeable* (positive, easygoing or pleasant)
   - *Disagree* (negative, expressing a different opinion)

Exercise 3: How Affixes Change Meaning

1. **Disinterested vs. Interested**
   - *Disinterested* means unbiased or impartial (neutral), whereas *interested* implies curiosity or concern (positive).
2. **Fearless vs. Fearful**
   - *Fearless* means without fear (positive, suggests bravery), while *fearful* means full of fear (negative, suggests apprehension).
3. **Encourage vs. Discourage**
   - *Encourage* (with *en-* prefix) means to inspire or support (positive), while *discourage* (with *dis-* prefix) means to dissuade or reduce confidence (negative).

Summary:
- **Affixes** can be *Prefixes* (in the beginning) and *Suffixes* (in

the end).
- **Positive Affixes** generally add meaning related to **goodness, ability, or quality,** like *-ful* (full of), *-ous* (full of), and *pro-* (in favor of).
- **Negative Affixes** are used to form words that convey a **lack of something** or **opposite qualities,** like *un-* (not), *dis-* (opposite of), and *-less* (without).

ROOT: "AQUA-" (MEANING: "WATER")

Vocabulary:
- **Aquatic:** Relating to water.
  Example: "The aquatic plants thrive in freshwater lakes."
- **Aqueduct:** A structure for conveying water.
  Example: "Ancient civilizations built aqueducts to bring water into cities."
- **Aqueous:** Something made of, like, or dissolved in water.
  Example: "The aqueous solution contained dissolved salts."

Additional Related Words:
- **Aquifer:** An underground layer of water-bearing rock.
  Example: "The town relied on the aquifer for its water supply."
- **Aquarium:** A container of water for fish, plants, etc.
  Example: "The aquarium houses various species of fish."
- **Aquaplane:** To glide over water on a board.
  Example: "They loved to aquaplane across the lake in summer."

Word Duel: *Aquatic vs. Terrestrial*
- Question: Which term best describes organisms that live primarily on land?
    - Aquatic

- - - Terrestrial
- **Correct Answer: <u>Terrestrial</u>**
  - Explanation: "**Aquatic**" refers to *water-based environments*, while "**Terrestrial**" refers to *land*.

Semantic Scale: Levels of Wetness
- *Damp*: Lightly wet (e.g., "The grass was <u>damp</u> with dew.")
- *Moist*: More humid than damp (e.g., "The soil was <u>moist</u> after the rain.")
- *Wet*: Fully covered in liquid (e.g., "The towels were <u>wet</u> from swimming.")
- *Soggy*: Unpleasantly saturated (e.g., "The papers became <u>soggy</u> in the rain.")
- *Drenched*: Completely soaked (e.g., "They were <u>drenched</u> from the downpour.")

Language Time Travel: "Aqua" and Its Evolution
- "Aquarium" comes from "aqua" combined with "-rium," a suffix implying a place or container. This term gained popularity in the 19th century with the creation of glass tanks to study marine life.

Synonyms and Antonyms
- **Aquatic**
  - *Synonym:* Marine (related to the sea or ocean).
  - *Antonym:* Terrestrial (referring to land).

ROOT: "-TERE-" (MEANING: "EARTH" OR "LAND")

Vocabulary:
- **Terrestrial:** Relating to or occurring on land.
  Example: "Forests, grasslands, and deserts are types of terrestrial ecosystems."
- **Territory:** A specific area of land, often under the control of a particular entity.
  Example: "The wolves defended their territory from rival packs."
- **Terrain:** The physical features or landscape of a region.
  Example: "The hikers were challenged by the rocky terrain."
- **Subterranean:** Existing or occurring below the earth's surface.
  Example: "The ancient city had subterranean tunnels used for water drainage."
- **Terrarium:** An enclosed space or container designed to mimic a terrestrial habitat for plants and animals.
  Example: "He created a terrarium with small plants and moss to keep on his desk."

Types of Terrain
- *Flatland*: Land that is largely level and free of high or low points.
- *Rolling Hills*: Land with gentle, moderate slopes.

- *Mountainous*: Land with steep and rugged elevations.
- *Rocky Terrain*: Land covered with rocks and uneven surfaces.
- *Desert*: A dry, barren land with sparse vegetation.

Language Time Travel: From "-Tere" to "Territory"

- The Latin root "-tere" or "terra," meaning "earth" or "land," has influenced words related to the land or areas of earth. "Territory" comes from the Latin "territorium," meaning a specific area of land. Over time, this root gave rise to words used to describe both the physical features of landscapes (terrain) and boundaries (territory).

Story: The Quest for the Hidden Oasis

Long ago, in a vast desert far from any town, there was a legend of a hidden oasis, a place where **aquatic** life thrived amidst the dry sands. It was said that this oasis was filled with crystal-clear **aqueous** pools surrounded by lush plants, a place of rare beauty in the otherwise barren **terrestrial** landscape.

Mira, a young explorer fascinated by both land and water, set out to find this hidden oasis. She traveled through harsh **terrain** for days, the **arid** environment testing her endurance. Along the way, she encountered strange **terrestrial** creatures, uniquely adapted to the dry climate. At night, she gazed up at the stars, dreaming of the cool, refreshing water that awaited her if she succeeded.

Finally, after a grueling journey, Mira stumbled upon the oasis. There, she found **aquatic** plants and small fish darting through the pools, their vibrant colors a striking contrast against the golden sand. She marveled at how this **aquatic** paradise had survived hidden within the **terrestrial** world of the desert.

Mira knew that she had found something precious, a place where **aqua** and **terra** met, forming a delicate balance. She spent days observing the unique ecosystem, grateful for the hidden wonders that nature holds when **water** and **land** come together.

ROOT: "VID-" OR "VIS-" (MEANING: "SEE" OR "LOOK")

Vocabulary:

1. **Video**: A recording of moving visual images.
Example: The teacher showed a short <u>video</u> to explain the lesson.

2. **Vision**: The ability to see or imagine something clearly.
Example: His <u>vision</u> for the future included a world with no poverty.

3. **Visual**: Related to seeing or sight.
Example: The <u>visual</u> effects in the movie were incredible.

4. **Evident**: Clear or obvious, easily seen.
Example: The damage from the storm was <u>evident</u> from the fallen trees and debris.

5. **Invisible**: Not able to be seen.
Example: The ghost was <u>invisible</u>, but its presence was felt in the room.

Word Duel: Vision vs. Invisible

Question: Which word refers to something that cannot be seen?

A) Vision
B) Invisible

Correct Answer: B) Invisible

Explanation: "Invisible" comes from the root "vid-" and refers to something that cannot be seen, while "vision" refers to the ability to see or imagine.

Semantic Scale: Levels of Seeing

This scale ranges from unclear or hard-to-see to clearly visible.

1. **Blurry** – Difficult to make out, unclear.

Example: The image on the screen was **blurry** due to the low resolution.

2. **Faint** – Slightly visible, not strong or clear.

Example: A **faint** glow could be seen in the distance.

3. **Clear** – Easily understood or seen.

Example: The instructions were **clear**, and everyone understood the task.

4. **Sharp** – Well-defined and distinct.

Example: His **sharp** eyesight allowed him to spot the deer from miles away.

5. **Obvious** – Easily seen or understood; unmistakable.

Example: The answer to the riddle was **obvious** once she explained it.

6. **Evident** – Clearly seen or understood.

Example: His nervousness was **evident** from the way he fidgeted.

Language Time Travel: Vision vs. Video

The word **vision** originally referred to the act of seeing, especially with clarity or purpose. Over time, it expanded to include imagination and foresight. On the other hand, **video** comes from the Latin word "videre," meaning "to see," but its use has evolved to describe recordings of what is seen.

Story: The Power of Sight

Lena had always been fascinated by how the world looked, not just in front of her eyes, but how people could imagine things beyond the **visible**. One day, her teacher showed a **video** in class that depicted the beauty of nature in slow motion. The **visual** effects were so lifelike that it felt like they could step right into the forest on the screen.

As Lena watched, she was reminded of her

own **vision** of the future—a world where nature and technology coexisted harmoniously. The **evidence** of progress was already **evident** in the small projects around her town. New buildings were designed with eco-friendly materials, and green spaces were being created everywhere.

However, one thing remained a mystery: the **invisible** forces that shaped these changes—like the environmental policies and the people behind the scenes—could not be seen directly, but their impact was clear. Lena smiled, knowing that what we cannot see is often the most powerful force driving change.

ROOT: "PHOBIA" (MEANING: "FEAR")

Vocabulary:
The root "phobia" refers to a fear of something, usually an irrational or excessive fear.

1. **Acrophobia**: The fear of heights.
   Example: She had acrophobia and couldn't even look out of tall windows.
2. **Cacophobia**: The fear of ugliness.
   Example: His irrational cacophobia caused him to avoid certain places.
3. **Claustrophobia**: The fear of confined spaces.
   Example: His claustrophobia made it difficult for him to ride in elevators.

Word Duel: Acrophobia vs. Claustrophobia
Question: Which word describes a fear of heights?
   A) Acrophobia
   B) Claustrophobia
Correct Answer: A) Acrophobia
Explanation: "Acrophobia" comes from the Greek "acro-" meaning "high" and "phobia" meaning "fear," describing the fear of heights, while "claustrophobia" is the fear of confined spaces.

Synonyms and Antonyms
   1. **Phobia**

- **Synonym**: Fear – Both words describe an emotional response to something that causes anxiety or dread.
- **Antonym**: Courage – Courage is the ability to face or overcome fear.

2. **Acrophobia**
   - **Synonym**: Heights fear – A fear of heights.
   - **Antonym**: Hypsophilia – A love of heights or high places.

Story: The Haunted House

The old mansion on the hill had always been a place of mystery. It was said to be evident that strange things happened there, as the lights would flicker and eerie sounds echoed through the walls at night. Jane, who had never believed in ghosts, dared to visit it, but her vision of the mansion became blurred with her rising **acrophobia** as she climbed the tall stairs. She noticed the invisible shadows of the past that seemed to haunt the rooms.

Meanwhile, Mark had a severe case of **claustrophobia**, so when they ventured into the small, locked attic, he began to panic. The house's eerie atmosphere made his fears worse, and it was obvious that his discomfort was growing. Despite the faint hopes of solving the mystery, Jane couldn't shake the feeling of malfunctioning logic. This experience was enough to make her rethink her approach to the unknown.

ROOT: "TRACT-" (MEANING: "PULL" OR "DRAG")

Vocabulary:
The root "tract-" refers to pulling, dragging, or drawing, and appears in words that relate to movement or force.

1. **Attract**: To draw something toward oneself.
   Example: The beautiful scenery seemed to <u>attract</u> tourists from all over the world.
2. **Contract**: To draw together, become smaller, or form an agreement.
   Example: He had to <u>contract</u> his muscles to lift the heavy weight.
3. **Distract**: To pull attention away from something.
   Example: The loud noise outside began to <u>distract</u> him from his work.
4. **Extract**: To pull something out, often with effort.
   Example: The dentist had to <u>extract</u> the broken tooth.
5. **Protract**: To draw out or extend in time.
   Example: The meeting seemed to <u>protract</u> well into the evening, making everyone tired.

Word Duel: Attract vs. Distract
Question: Which word describes drawing something towards you?
   A) Attract
   B) Distract

Correct Answer: A) Attract

Explanation: "Attract" comes from the root "tract-" meaning "to draw" and refers to the action of pulling something towards you, while "distract" involves pulling attention away from something.

Semantic Scale: Levels of Attention

This scale shows words ranging from fully focused attention to complete diversion.

1. **Focus** – Full concentration on something.

   Example: She needed to **focus** on her exam to get the best results.

2. **Engage** – To hold one's attention, often actively.

   Example: The story **engaged** the audience from start to finish.

3. **Concentrate** – To focus attention and effort on one thing.

   Example: He had to **concentrate** hard to solve the challenging puzzle.

4. **Divert** – To change focus or direction.

   Example: The sound of the siren **diverted** his attention away from the task.

5. **Distract** – To pull attention away, causing lack of focus.

   Example: The bright lights outside began to **distract** me while I was studying.

6. **Oblivious** – Completely unaware, no focus.

   Example: He was so **oblivious** to his surroundings that he didn't notice the storm approaching.

Language Time Travel: Contract vs. Protract

The word **contract** comes from the Latin "contractus," meaning "to pull together" or "tighten." It is used to describe things becoming smaller or an agreement being made. **Protract**, on the other hand, comes from "protractus," meaning "to draw out," and is used when something is extended over time.

Story: The Power of Movement

One afternoon, Sarah and her friends decided to hike up a mountain. The stunning view from the peak would **attract** people from miles away, making it a popular spot for nature lovers. As they reached the base, they noticed how the trail seemed to **contract** as it narrowed between the rocks, forcing them to squeeze through tight spaces.

Halfway up, Sarah's mind began to wander. The chirping birds and rustling leaves **distracted** her from the climb, and she almost lost her footing. Her friend, Jake, called her attention back to the path, making her focus again.

As they finally reached the top, the view seemed to **extract** all their worries, replacing them with a sense of peace. But their joy was interrupted when the sky darkened, threatening rain. With no time to waste, they decided to **protract** their hike by taking a longer route down, ensuring they would avoid the coming storm.

In the end, they realized how the mountain had taught them to balance attention and focus—to draw things in, let go when necessary, and extend their efforts when time was short.

ROOT: "MORPH" (MEANING: "FORM" OR "SHAPE")

Vocabulary:
The root "morph" refers to form or shape and is often used in words related to physical changes or transformations.

1. **Metamorphosis**: A complete change of form or structure.

    Example: The caterpillar underwent a <u>metamorphosis</u> and became a butterfly.

2. **Morphology**: The study of the form or structure of things, especially words or organisms.

    Example: She was fascinated by the <u>morphology</u> of different languages.

3. **Anthropomorphize**: To attribute human characteristics to something non-human.

    Example: The cartoon animals were <u>anthropomorphized</u>, with human-like speech and behaviors.

4. **Amorphous**: Lacking a clear shape or form.

    Example: The jellyfish had an <u>amorphous</u> body that floated aimlessly in the water.

Word Duel: Metamorphosis vs. Amorphous
Question: Which word refers to something with a clear, defined form?
   A) Metamorphosis
   B) Amorphous

Correct Answer: A) Metamorphosis
Explanation: "Metamorphosis" refers to a complete transformation, often with a clear and distinct form in the final state, while "amorphous" describes something that lacks a defined shape or form.

Synonyms and Antonyms
1. **Morphology**
   - **Synonym**: Form – Both words refer to the structure or shape of something.
   - **Antonym**: Disorder – Disorder refers to a lack of structure or organization.
2. **Metamorphosis**
   - **Synonym**: Transformation – Both refer to a significant change in form or appearance.
   - **Antonym**: Stasis – Refers to no change or movement.

Story: The Changing Landscape

In the quiet village, the weather seemed to attract travelers who came to enjoy the peaceful surroundings. However, as the years passed, the town began to contract in size, with fewer businesses and fewer visitors. The once bustling streets were now distracted by the construction of new highways that cut through the heart of the town. Some locals were saddened by the change, while others saw it as an opportunity for growth.

One artist, who had always seen the beauty in the town's **morphology**, tried to extract the essence of its original charm through his paintings. The village seemed to undergo a **metamorphosis**, as new modern structures were built alongside the old. Yet, despite the changes, it was clear that the town's heart was still intact, albeit in a more **amorphous** form.

ROOT: "SCRIB-" OR "SCRIPT-" (MEANING: "WRITE")

Vocabulary:
The root "scrib-" or "script-" comes from Latin and refers to writing or recording.

1. **Describe**: To give an account or representation of something in words.

    Example: The witness was able to <u>describe</u> the suspect to the police with great detail.

2. **Script**: The written text of a play, movie, or speech.

    Example: The actors rehearsed their <u>script</u> before the play's opening night.

3. **Inscription**: Words that are carved, engraved, or written on something, especially a monument.

    Example: The <u>inscription</u> on the plaque commemorated the founding of the city.

4. **Transcribe**: To write down or copy something, especially spoken words.

    Example: She had to <u>transcribe</u> the meeting minutes into a report.

5. **Subscribe**: To sign up for something, such as a service or publication.

    Example: I decided to <u>subscribe</u> to the magazine for a year to get the latest updates.

Word Duel: Describe vs. Transcribe

Question: Which word refers to copying something written or spoken?
   A) Describe
   B) Transcribe

Correct Answer: B) Transcribe

Explanation: "Transcribe" comes from the root "scrib-" and means to write down or copy something, often verbatim. "Describe" involves expressing the details of something, often in a narrative way.

Semantic Scale: Levels of Writing

This scale shows words related to the act of writing, ranging from recording exact words to creative description.

1. **Note** – A brief, written message.

   Example: He wrote a **note** to remind himself about the meeting.

2. **Jot** – To write quickly or in a brief manner.

   Example: She **jotted** down her thoughts in the notebook before heading out.

3. **Describe** – To give an account of something, often in detail.

   Example: Can you **describe** what the suspect looked like?

4. **Transcribe** – To write something out, often word for word.

   Example: She had to **transcribe** the interview for her research paper.

5. **Compose** – To create or write something, especially a piece of music or literature.

   Example: The author sat down to **compose** her new novel.

6. **Author** – To write or create a piece of work, typically a book.

   Example: She is the **author** of several bestselling novels.

Language Time Travel: Script vs. Inscription

The word **script** originates from the Latin "scriptus," meaning "written." It was originally used to refer to handwritten documents and later evolved to mean any written text, such as plays or screenplays. **Inscription** comes from the Latin "inscriptio," which means "to write on." It refers to words that are engraved or carved, often on monuments or memorials.

Story: The Power of Words

Liam was an aspiring playwright, and his latest project was a historical drama about a famous local hero. He worked late into the night, trying to **describe** the hero's journey with vivid detail, aiming to capture the essence of their courage and determination. As he worked, his mind turned to the **script**, which he had been refining for weeks. It had to be perfect for the upcoming play.

One afternoon, he visited a monument dedicated to the hero. As he walked around, he noticed the **inscription** on the stone, honoring the hero's legacy. It was a simple but powerful message that would forever memorialize their deeds. Inspired by this, Liam decided to **transcribe** the **inscription** into his **script**, hoping to honor the hero in a way that future generations could remember.

As he sat down at his desk, he realized the importance of his words, knowing that just as people **subscribe** to newspapers or newsletters, they would one day **subscribe** to the ideas his play communicated. Writing, he thought, was a powerful way to leave a legacy, just like the **inscription** on the monument that had moved him so deeply.

ROOT: "TECHNO" (MEANING: "ART" OR "SKILL")

Vocabulary:

The root "techno" relates to art, skill, or craft, especially in areas that involve specialized knowledge or machinery.

1. **Technology**: The use of scientific knowledge for practical purposes.

    Example: Advances in technology have transformed the way we communicate.

2. **Technique**: A method or way of doing something, especially one requiring skill.

    Example: The artist demonstrated her unique painting technique to the students.

3. **Technician**: A person skilled in a particular craft or technical field.

    Example: The technician fixed the broken computer in no time.

4. **Techniques**: Methods or skills used to accomplish a task.

    Example: The chef used various techniques to create the perfect dish.

5. **Biotechnology**: The use of living organisms or biological systems in technology.

    Example: Biotechnology has played a crucial role in advancements in medicine.

Word Duel: Technology vs. Technique

Question: Which word refers to the application of scientific knowledge to solve problems?
 A) Technology
 B) Technique

Correct Answer: A) Technology

Explanation: "Technology" comes from the root "techno" and refers to the use of scientific and technical knowledge to solve problems and create tools. "Technique," on the other hand, refers to the method or way something is done, often requiring skill.

Synonyms and Antonyms

1. **Technology**
    - **Synonym**: Innovation – Both refer to the application of new methods or inventions.
    - **Antonym**: Obsolescence – The state of being outdated or no longer in use.
2. **Technique**
    - **Synonym**: Method – A systematic way of doing something.
    - **Antonym**: Ineptness – Lack of skill or ability.

Story: The Invention of the Future

In a small town, the rapid advancements in **technology** had begun to change the way people lived. The local library, once filled with shelves of books, was now equipped with the latest **technological** innovations, including virtual reality stations and 3D printers. The town's **technicians** worked hard to ensure that the systems ran smoothly.

One young inventor, inspired by the **techniques** of the past, wanted to create a device that would allow people to **transcribe** their thoughts into written text. His plan was to merge old and new, taking the ancient art of writing and combining it with cutting-edge **technology**. As he worked tirelessly, he reflected on how the most innovative ideas often come from the simplest **descriptions** of what people need.

ROOT: "VOC-" OR "VOK-" (MEANING: "CALL" OR "VOICE")

Vocabulary:
The root "voc-" or "vok-" comes from Latin and relates to calling, voicing, or speaking out.

1. **Vocal**: Relating to the voice; expressing opinions openly.

   Example: She was very <u>vocal</u> about her support for the new policy.

2. **Invoke**: To call upon something, especially for help or inspiration.

   Example: The poet would often <u>invoke</u> nature as a source of inspiration.

3. **Revoke**: To take back or withdraw.

   Example: His driver's license was <u>revoked</u> after repeated offenses.

4. **Advocate**: To speak in favor of something or someone; a person who supports a cause.

   Example: She is an <u>advocate</u> for environmental protection and sustainability.

5. **Provoke**: To stir up, arouse, or call forth a reaction.

   Example: His rude comments were meant to <u>provoke</u> a reaction from the crowd.

Word Duel: Invoke vs. Provoke
Question: Which word means to call upon something for

support or inspiration?
   A) Invoke
   B) Provoke

Correct Answer: A) Invoke

Explanation: "Invoke" comes from the root "voc-" and means to call upon something or someone, often for support, inspiration, or authority. "Provoke," on the other hand, means to incite or stir up a reaction, often negative.

Semantic Scale: Levels of Support

This scale shows words related to different levels and types of support or advocacy.

1. **Suggest** – To put forth an idea or proposal mildly.
   Example: She **suggested** trying a new approach to the project.

2. **Encourage** – To give support and confidence.
   Example: His teacher **encouraged** him to pursue his talent in art.

3. **Advise** – To offer guidance or counsel.
   Example: She was asked to **advise** the new team members on their roles.

4. **Advocate** – To actively support or defend a cause or person.
   Example: The organization **advocates** for equal rights and opportunities.

5. **Champion** – To fight vigorously for a cause or on behalf of someone.
   Example: He became a **champion** for children's health and nutrition.

Language Time Travel: Vocal vs. Invoke

The word **vocal** comes from the Latin "vocalis," meaning "speaking or calling out," and is used to describe someone who speaks openly or relates to the voice. **Invoke** originates from the Latin "invocare," meaning "to call upon." It suggests calling forth something, usually as support, inspiration, or authority, adding a sense of formality or reverence.

Story: The Power of Words

Amelia had always been a **vocal** supporter of animal rights. She wasn't afraid to **advocate** for the cause, speaking at rallies and writing articles to raise awareness. One day, during a protest, she had to **invoke** the memory of a beloved animal sanctuary that had recently closed due to funding issues. The story helped inspire the crowd and reignited their passion for the cause.

However, her powerful words had consequences. A local politician, who disagreed with her views, tried to **provoke** her by making dismissive remarks. Amelia knew that she had to stay calm and focused. She didn't let his words **revoke** her determination but instead used the moment to speak more passionately than ever about the importance of protecting animals and preserving their habitats.

In the end, Amelia realized that using her **vocal** voice in the right way could bring real change and motivate others to join her mission.

ROOT: "PATH-" (MEANING: "FEELING" OR "SUFFERING")

Vocabulary:
The root "path-" refers to feeling, suffering, or disease and is used in words that relate to emotions or conditions.

1. **Sympathy**: The feeling of compassion or understanding for someone else's suffering.

    Example: She felt <u>sympathy</u> for her friend who had lost a loved one.

2. **Empathy**: The ability to understand and share the feelings of another.

    Example: A good therapist shows <u>empathy</u> to help clients feel understood.

3. **Apathy**: Lack of interest or concern.

    Example: His <u>apathy</u> toward current events surprised his friends.

4. **Pathology**: The study of diseases or the condition of a particular disease.

    Example: She decided to study <u>pathology</u> to better understand illness and treatment.

5. **Psychopath**: A person with a severe personality disorder characterized by a lack of empathy.

    Example: The character in the book was portrayed as a

psychopath with no remorse for his actions.

Word Duel: Sympathy vs. Apathy

Question: Which word refers to a lack of interest or concern?

A) Sympathy
B) Apathy

Correct Answer: B) Apathy

Explanation: "Apathy" comes from the root "path-" and means a lack of feeling or interest. "Sympathy" implies sharing or understanding another's feelings.

Synonyms and Antonyms

1. **Sympathy**
   - **Synonym**: Compassion – Both words refer to feeling concern for others.
   - **Antonym**: Indifference – Lack of interest or concern.

2. **Advocate**
   - **Synonym**: Supporter – A person who backs or promotes a cause.
   - **Antonym**: Opponent – Someone who disagrees with or resists a cause.

Story: The Impact of Understanding Emotions

Lena had always been a compassionate person, and she felt **sympathy** for those who were struggling. When her friend lost a family member, Lena reached out to offer her support, understanding the depth of her friend's grief. As a psychology student, Lena knew the importance of **empathy** in helping others heal. She spent time listening to her friend's pain, truly connecting with her feelings.

However, there was one person in her life who seemed distant and indifferent—her coworker, Mark. His constant **apathy** toward anything happening around him baffled Lena. He seemed uninterested in the world, ignoring even the most pressing issues that affected their community.

Curious about his behavior, Lena decided to learn more about **pathology** and how certain conditions could influence a person's emotions. It was then that she encountered the term **psychopath**, which helped her understand why Mark might lack the ability to relate to others' feelings. Unlike her own **empathy**, Mark seemed disconnected from the human experience of compassion.

This made Lena reflect on the vast differences in how people experience emotions and how important it is to foster **sympathy** and **empathy** in the world.

ROOT: "AUTO-" (MEANING: "SELF")

Vocabulary:
The root "auto-" comes from Greek and means self or same.

1. **Autonomy**: The condition of being self-governing or independent.

   Example: The country achieved <u>autonomy</u> after years of colonial rule.

2. **Autograph**: A person's own signature, especially one written as a personal memento.

   Example: She asked for his <u>autograph</u> after his speech.

3. **Automobile**: A vehicle powered by its own engine, typically a car.

   Example: The new <u>automobile</u> model is more fuel-efficient than its predecessor.

4. **Automatic**: Operating without human intervention; happening by itself.

   Example: The lights in the room turn on <u>automatically</u> when you enter.

5. **Autobiography**: The story of a person's life written by that person.

   Example: He wrote an <u>autobiography</u> to share his experiences with the world.

Word Duel: Autograph vs. Autobiography

Question: Which word refers to the story of a person's life

written by that person?
A) Autograph
B) Autobiography

Correct Answer: B) Autobiography

Explanation: "Autobiography" comes from the root "auto-" and refers to a self-written account of one's life. "Autograph" refers to a person's own signature, often given to others as a keepsake.

Synonyms and Antonyms

1. **Autonomy**
   - **Synonym**: Independence – The state of being self-sufficient or free.
   - **Antonym**: Dependence – The state of relying on others for support or guidance.

2. **Automatic**
   - **Synonym**: Instinctive – Acting without conscious thought or direction.
   - **Antonym**: Manual – Requiring physical effort or intervention.

Story: The Power of Self-Determination

In a thriving city, a young entrepreneur built an **automobile** company that emphasized **autonomy** in its design and operation. Each vehicle was engineered to be fully **automatic**, running with minimal human intervention. One of the company's founders, who had written his own **autobiography**, became a role model for aspiring business leaders, proving that self-determination could lead to great success.

Meanwhile, a local artist who loved collecting **autographs** had decided to write her own story and include it in her upcoming exhibition. Her **autonomy** in choosing to represent herself in this personal way gave her a unique sense of ownership and pride.

ROOT: - "TELE-" (MEANING: "FAR" OR "DISTANT")

Vocabulary:
The root "tele-" comes from Greek and refers to something that is far off, distant, or operating over a distance.

1. **Telephone**: A device used for transmitting voice over long distances.

    Example: She used her <u>telephone</u> to call her friend who lived overseas.

2. **Television**: A device for receiving and transmitting moving images and sound over a distance.

    Example: They watched their favorite show on <u>television</u>.

3. **Telescope**: A tool used to observe distant objects, usually in space.

    Example: The astronomer used a <u>telescope</u> to study distant stars.

4. **Telepathy**: The ability to communicate through thought alone, without using words or physical signals.

    Example: The two psychics claimed to have the power of <u>telepathy</u>.

5. **Teleport**: To transport something instantaneously from one place to another.

    Example: In science fiction, characters often <u>teleport</u>

from one planet to another.

Word Duel: Telepathy vs. Teleport
Question: Which word refers to the ability to communicate using only thoughts, with no physical interaction?
    A) Telepathy
    B) Teleport
Correct Answer: A) Telepathy
Explanation: "Telepathy" comes from the root "tele-" and refers to the transmission of thoughts from one mind to another without the use of any physical senses. "Teleport" refers to the act of moving from one place to another instantly, typically using technology or supernatural means.

Synonyms and Antonyms
1. **Television**
   - **Synonym**: TV – A common, informal way to refer to a television.
   - **Antonym**: Radio – A device used for transmitting sound but not visual content.
2. **Telephone**
   - **Synonym**: Phone – A more informal term for a telephone.
   - **Antonym**: Silence – The absence of sound or communication.

Story: The Communication Revolution

    In the past, people had to rely on **telegrams** to communicate over long distances. Now, technology has advanced so far that we can talk to someone using a **telephone**, or watch a program from anywhere in the world on **television**. The advent of the **telephone** revolutionized the way people communicated, and the **television** made it possible to see what was happening in distant places. One day, scientists hoped to use **telepathy** to enhance communication, eliminating the need for any physical devices. As technology continues to evolve, we may even be able to **teleport** from one place to another in the blink of an eye.

ROOT: "THERM-" (MEANING : "HEAT")

Vocabulary:
The root "therm-" comes from Greek and relates to heat or temperature.

1. **Thermometer**: An instrument used to measure temperature.

    Example: The <u>thermometer</u> read 90°F, signaling a hot day.

2. **Thermal**: Related to heat.

    Example: The building had <u>thermal</u> insulation to keep it warm in the winter.

3. **Endothermic**: Refers to a process or reaction that absorbs heat.

    Example: The <u>endothermic</u> reaction caused the test tube to feel cold to the touch.

4. **Exothermic**: Refers to a process or reaction that releases heat.

    Example: The <u>exothermic</u> reaction in the test tube caused the surrounding air to warm up.

5. **Hypothermia**: A dangerous condition caused by extremely low body temperature.

    Example: The hiker suffered from <u>hypothermia</u> after being stranded in the snow for hours.

Word Duel: Exothermic vs. Endothermic

Question: Which word refers to a process that absorbs heat?
  A) Exothermic
  B) Endothermic

Correct Answer: B) Endothermic

Explanation: "Endothermic" refers to a process that absorbs heat (e.g., a chemical reaction), while "exothermic" refers to processes that release heat.

Semantic Scale: Temperature-Related Terms

This scale shows words related to temperature, ranging from cold to hot:

1. **Freezing** – Extremely cold, below 32°F (0°C).
   Example: The water was **freezing** when I touched it, so I quickly pulled my hand away.

2. **Cold** – Below normal temperature.
   Example: The **cold** wind made it feel like winter had arrived early.

3. **Cool** – Slightly cold or refreshing.
   Example: She enjoyed a **cool** breeze on the summer evening.

4. **Warm** – Slightly hot, pleasant.
   Example: The weather was **warm** enough for a walk in the park.

5. **Hot** – High in temperature.
   Example: It was so **hot** that we decided to stay indoors.

6. **Scorching** – Extremely hot, often uncomfortably so.
   Example: The **scorching** heat of the desert made traveling difficult.

Language Time Travel: Thermometer vs. Hypothermia

The word **thermometer** comes from the Greek roots "therme" (heat) and "metron" (measure), originally used to measure the heat of water. Over time, it evolved to measure the temperature of air, bodies, and objects. **Hypothermia**, on the other hand, comes from the Greek "hypo" (under) and "therme" (heat), meaning "below heat," describing a dangerously low body temperature.

Story: The Science of Heat

One summer afternoon, Emma decided to take a walk in the park. She checked the **thermometer** before heading out and saw that the temperature had already reached 90°F. It was going to be a **thermal** challenge, but she was excited to enjoy the sunshine.

As she walked, she remembered a science experiment she had conducted in school. She recalled an **endothermic** reaction, where the chemicals in the test tube absorbed heat, making the outside feel cooler. It fascinated her how energy could be drawn in and used.

Later, while hiking, Emma noticed something strange. She had read about **exothermic** reactions before, where heat is released, but this time it was something different. A sudden storm made the air feel much colder, and she began to feel chills. When she reached the cabin, the temperature inside was so cold that she realized she was suffering from **hypothermia**. Fortunately, after warming up, she was okay, but she learned the hard way how heat, whether absorbed or released, could have such powerful effects on the body.

ROOT: "PORT-" (MEANING: "CARRY")

Vocabulary:

The root "port-" comes from Latin and relates to carrying, transporting, or moving something from one place to another.

1. **Transport**: To carry something from one place to another.

   Example: The goods were transported across the country by train.

2. **Portable**: Able to be easily carried or moved.

   Example: The portable speaker is perfect for taking to the beach.

3. **Import**: To bring goods or services into a country from abroad.

   Example: The company decided to import rare wines from France.

4. **Export**: To send goods or services to another country for sale.

   Example: The country exports textiles to markets all over the world.

5. **Portion**: A part or share of something, often referring to food.

   Example: I had a small portion of salad with my meal.

Word Duel: Import vs. Export

Question: Which word refers to bringing goods into a country

from abroad?
A) Import
B) Export

Correct Answer: A) Import

Explanation: "Import" comes from the root "port-" and refers to the action of bringing goods or services into a country. "Export" refers to sending goods or services to other countries.

Semantic Scale: Levels of Carrying

This scale shows words related to carrying, from light transportation to significant movement:

1. **Carry** – To hold and transport something from one place to another.

   Example: I had to **carry** my bags all the way home.

2. **Transport** – To move something from one place to another, often by a vehicle.

   Example: The company uses trucks to **transport** goods.

3. **Convey** – To make something known or to transport it in a more formal sense.

   Example: The speech was designed to **convey** the importance of unity.

4. **Transfer** – To move from one place to another, especially when changing ownership or position.

   Example: She decided to **transfer** her credits to another university.

5. **Import** – To bring goods or services into a country.

   Example: The country **imports** luxury items from around the world.

6. **Export** – To send goods or services to another country.

   Example: The region **exports** its agricultural products to neighboring nations.

Language Time Travel: Portable vs. Transport

The word **portable** comes from the Latin "portare" (to carry) and "abilis" (able), describing something that can be easily carried. **Transport** comes from "trans" (across) and "portare" (to carry), originally referring to the act of carrying something across distances. Over time, both terms retained their connection to the act of carrying but evolved into specific contexts like mobility and movement.

Story: The Journey of Trade

In a small port city, goods were constantly **transported** from one place to another, with merchants **importing** fine silk from the East and **exporting** local pottery to foreign lands. One merchant carried a **portable** device that helped him keep track of shipments. He knew that his **portion** of the profits would depend on how well he managed to move goods efficiently across borders. Every trade journey was an exercise in mastering the art of **importing** and **exporting**.

ROOT: "SUB-" (MEANING: "UNDER" OR "BELOW")

Vocabulary:
The root "sub-" comes from Latin and means "under," "below," or "beneath." It's used in many English words that indicate something is under something else or lower in position.

1. **Submarine**: A vessel designed to operate underwater.

Example: The crew aboard the <u>submarine</u> explored the ocean depths.

2. **Subterranean**: Existing or occurring beneath the surface of the earth.

Example: The ancient city had <u>subterranean</u> tunnels used for escape.

3. **Subdue**: To overpower, bring under control, or reduce in intensity.

Example: The police were able to <u>subdue</u> the suspect without injury.

4. **Subscript**: A small number or letter written beneath or after a symbol, often used in mathematics or chemistry.

Example: The <u>subscript</u> "2" in H_2O represents the number of hydrogen atoms.

5. **Subordinate**: Lower in rank, position, or importance;

someone who is under the authority of another.

Example: He was a subordinate in the company, reporting directly to the CEO.

Word Duel: Subordinate vs. Superior

Question: Which word describes someone who holds a lower rank or position?

   A) Subordinate
   B) Superior

Correct Answer: A) Subordinate

Explanation: "Subordinate" comes from the root "sub-" meaning "under," and refers to someone in a lower rank or position. "Superior" is the opposite, indicating a higher rank.

Semantic Scale: Levels of Being Below or Under

This scale shows words related to being under or below, with increasing levels of depth or inferiority:

1. **Under** – Below something in position or level.
   Example: The keys are **under** the book.
2. **Sub-** – A prefix meaning "below" or "under," often used in more formal contexts.
   Example: The workers entered the **sub**level of the building.
3. **Beneath** – A more formal or poetic term meaning directly under or below.
   Example: He placed the box **beneath** the table.
4. **Subterranean** – Beneath the earth's surface; underground.
   Example: The old ruins were hidden in a **subterranean** chamber.
5. **Inferior** – Lower in rank, quality, or importance.
   Example: He felt **inferior** to his colleagues in terms of experience.

Language Time Travel: Submarine vs. Subterranean

The word **submarine** comes from Latin "sub" (under) and "marinus" (sea), referring to a vessel designed to operate **under** the sea. **Subterranean** comes from Latin "sub" (under) and "terra" (earth), referring to something that exists **beneath** the earth's surface.

Story: Adventures Beneath the Surface

Captain Riley commanded the **submarine** that was tasked with exploring the deep ocean. As the vessel descended, the crew marveled at the **subterranean** world that lay beneath them, filled with mysterious creatures and unseen landscapes. They were diving into a part of the ocean few had ever seen, and the silence was almost overwhelming.

However, the calm was broken when the submarine's systems started to malfunction. Riley had to **subdue** his rising panic and focus on finding a solution. He knew he had to remain calm to avoid worsening the situation.

Back at the surface, the engineers worked furiously, using their expertise to fix the problem. The submarine's systems were repaired just in time, and Riley looked over the report, noting a **subscript** in the chemical analysis of the water sample, which provided vital information. He then made a note in his log, making sure to check the ranks and positions of his team members, understanding that despite their challenges, they were all **subordinate** to one ultimate goal: a safe return to the surface.

By the end of the journey, the crew had successfully completed their mission, proving that even in the depths of the ocean, teamwork and composure are key.

ROOT: "AUD-" (MEANING: "HEAR" OR "LISTEN")

Vocabulary:
The root "aud-" comes from Latin, meaning "to hear" or "to listen." It is the foundation of many words related to sound and hearing.

1. **Audience**: A group of people who gather to watch or listen to something.

   Example: The **audience** cheered loudly after the final performance.

2. **Audible**: Capable of being heard.

   Example: The noise from the construction site was barely **audible** through the thick walls.

3. **Audio**: Related to sound, especially the recording or reproduction of sound.

   Example: He connected the **audio** system to the speakers for the party.

4. **Audition**: A trial performance to evaluate someone's ability, especially in acting or music.

   Example: She prepared for her **audition** by rehearsing her lines.

5. **Audit**: An official inspection of financial accounts or records, derived from "to hear," originally meaning to listen to accounts.

   Example: The company will have an **audit** of its financial statements next month.

Word Duel: Audible vs. Invisible
Question: Which word refers to something that can be heard?
   A) Audible
   B) Invisible
Correct Answer: A) Audible
Explanation: "Audible" comes from the root "aud-," meaning "to hear," and refers to something that can be heard. "Invisible" refers to something that cannot be seen, derived from "vis-," meaning "to see."

Levels of Hearing
This shows words related to hearing, from the ability to hear sounds to specific actions involving listening:

1. **Hear** – To perceive sound through the ear.
   Example: Did you **hear** that noise?
2. **Listen** – To pay attention to sound deliberately.
   Example: I love to **listen** to music while working.
3. **Audible** – Able to be heard.
   Example: The sound was just barely **audible** in the room.
4. **Auditory** – Related to hearing or the sense of hearing.
   Example: The doctor performed an **auditory** test to check for hearing issues.
5. **Audition** – A trial performance to assess one's talent in music, acting, etc.
   Example: He was nervous for his **audition** but gave an impressive performance.

Language Time Travel: Audience vs. Auditory
The word **audience** comes from the Latin word "audientia," meaning "a group of listeners," which stems from "audire" (to hear). Similarly, **auditory** is derived from "auditus," meaning "hearing," and refers to anything related to the sense of hearing. Over time, both terms maintained their focus on hearing but evolved into more specific uses—one for people who listen (audience) and the other for the sense itself (auditory).

Story: The Big Performance

It was the night of the annual school talent show, and the **audience** filled the auditorium, eager to see the performances. The lights dimmed, and the first act took the stage. As the music played, the sound was **audible** even in the back row, and everyone could feel the energy in the air.

Behind the scenes, Sarah was preparing for her **audition**. She had worked for weeks to perfect her performance and was determined to impress the judges. As the clock ticked down, she took a deep breath, ensuring the **audio** system was set up perfectly for her song.

When her turn came, she stepped onto the stage, giving it her all. The judges watched closely, listening carefully to her voice. After the performance, she anxiously waited for feedback. The judges were impressed, but before they made their decision, the school accountant entered to perform an **audit** of the event's finances. He ensured everything was in order before the final decision was made.

In the end, Sarah's hard work paid off, and she was selected as the winner, grateful for the opportunity to showcase her talent in front of such an enthusiastic **audience**.

ROOT: "PHIL-" (MEANING: "LOVE" OR "AFFINITY FOR")

Vocabulary:

The Greek root "phil-" means "love" or "affinity for" and appears in words that convey a strong liking or passion for something.

1. **Philosophy**: The study of fundamental truths about knowledge, existence, and values; literally, "love of wisdom."

Example: She decided to study philosophy to explore life's biggest questions.

2. **Philology**: The study of language and its history; literally, "love of words."

Example: His passion for ancient texts led him to a career in philology.

3. **Philanthropy**: The desire to promote the welfare of others, often through charitable acts; literally, "love of humanity."

Example: The foundation engages in philanthropy to support education and healthcare.

4. **Bibliophile**: A person who loves or collects books.

Example: As a true bibliophile, she spent most weekends exploring bookstores.

5. **Philharmonic**: Pertaining to a love of music, often referring to a symphony orchestra or musical society.
Example: They attended a philharmonic concert to hear a live performance of classical music.

Word Duel: Philology vs. Bibliophile
Question: Which word refers to a person who loves books?
A) Philology
B) Bibliophile
Correct Answer: B) Bibliophile
Explanation: "Bibliophile" combines "biblio" (book) with "phil-" (love), describing a person who has a love for or collects books. "Philology," however, refers to the love of language and the study of its history.

Semantic Scale: Levels of Love or Passion for Something
This scale shows words related to love or passion, with each term expressing a different type of affinity or enthusiasm.

1. **Interest** – A mild liking or curiosity about something.
Example: He had an **interest** in gardening.
2. **Affinity** – A natural liking for something, often with a feeling of connection.
Example: She had an **affinity** for languages and quickly picked them up.
3. **Enthusiasm** – Great interest or excitement for a particular activity or subject.
Example: His **enthusiasm** for cooking was contagious.
4. **Passion** – An intense, deeply felt liking or dedication to something.
Example: Her **passion** for art was evident in every painting.
5. **Philosophy** – The love and pursuit of wisdom, typically through systematic thought.
Example: He had a **philosophy** of living a meaningful and reflective life.
6. **Philanthropy** – A profound love for humanity, often shown through charitable actions.

Example: **Philanthropy** motivated him to donate his fortune to build schools.

Language Time Travel: Philosophy vs. Philanthropy
The word **philosophy** comes from Greek roots "philo-" (love) and "sophia" (wisdom), literally meaning "love of wisdom." **Philanthropy** combines "philo-" with "anthropos" (human), referring to a "love of humanity" that inspires charitable actions. Over time, these terms kept their emphasis on a love for something but evolved into disciplines and actions dedicated to people, ideas, and community support.

Story: The Gift of Giving

Anna had always been a lover of learning, so when she entered college, she decided to major in **philosophy**. She was fascinated by the deep questions about existence and the pursuit of wisdom. One day, while reading an ancient text, she discovered the term **philology** and became intrigued by the study of language and its rich history. Inspired, she added a second major to explore the evolution of words and languages throughout time.

Beyond academics, Anna had a heart for helping others. She admired her grandmother's passion for **philanthropy** and decided to start a charity focused on providing educational resources to underprivileged children. She believed in the power of giving back and wanted to make a difference in the world.

In her free time, Anna was a proud **bibliophile**, spending hours in local bookstores searching for rare and antique books. She often found solace in the pages of novels, and her collection grew with each passing year.

One evening, Anna attended a **philharmonic** concert at the city's grand hall. As she sat in awe of the orchestra's performance, she realized that her love for learning, language, giving, books, and music was all connected by one common thread: a deep passion for the things that enrich the human experience.

ROOT: "GEO-" (MEANING: "EARTH" OR "GROUND")

Vocabulary:

The Greek root "geo-" means "earth" or "ground" and is the basis for words that describe aspects of the physical earth or the study of the earth.

1. **Geography**: The study of the earth's physical features, climates, and resources.

    Example: She took a course in geography to understand how different landscapes are formed.

2. **Geology**: The scientific study of the earth's structure and the processes that have shaped it over time.

    Example: His interest in rocks led him to a career in geology.

3. **Geothermal**: Related to heat originating within the earth.

    Example: Geothermal energy is harnessed to provide a sustainable power source in some regions.

4. **Geometry**: The branch of mathematics concerned with shapes, sizes, and the properties of space (originally measuring earth and land).

    Example: In ancient times, geometry was used to divide land and calculate distances.

5. **Geopolitical**: Related to politics, especially in relation to geographical factors.
Example: The country's geopolitical position made it strategically important in international relations.

Word Duel: Geology vs. Geography
Question: Which word refers to the study of the earth's physical features, climates, and resources?
A) Geology
B) Geography
Correct Answer: B) Geography
Explanation: "Geography" focuses on studying the earth's physical features and landscapes. "Geology," on the other hand, is the study of the earth's structure, rocks, and the processes that shape it.

Semantic Scale: Levels of Earth Study and Interaction
This scale covers different areas of earth-related study, from general geography to highly specialized fields.

Topography – The detailed mapping or description of the features of an area.
Example: The mountain's **topography** was mapped out for hikers.

Geography – The study of physical features and resources of the earth.
Example: **Geography** covers everything from climate zones to ecosystems.

Geology – The study of the earth's physical structure and substance.
Example: In **geology**, scientists study rock formations and fossils.

Geophysics – The study of physical processes and properties of the earth.
Example: **Geophysics** can help predict earthquakes and other natural events.

Geopolitics – The influence of geography on politics, especially regarding territorial relations.

Example: **Geopolitics** plays a major role in decisions about natural resources and borders.

Language Time Travel: Geography vs. Geology
Geography comes from the Greek roots "geo" (earth) and "graphia" (writing or description), meaning "writing about the earth." **Geology**, on the other hand, combines "geo" with "logia" (study of), meaning "the study of the earth." Over time, **geography** became known as the study of the earth's surface and features, while **geology** focused more on what lies beneath the surface and the earth's physical makeup.

Story: Exploring the Earth

As a young girl, Mia was fascinated by the world around her, especially the diverse landscapes that stretched as far as the eye could see. She took an interest in **geography** early on, curious about how mountains, rivers, and deserts were formed and how climates varied across the globe. When she entered college, Mia decided to study **geology**, hoping to understand the earth's structure and the natural processes that shaped its features over millions of years.

One day, while visiting a geothermal plant, Mia was amazed to see **geothermal** energy being used to generate electricity from heat deep beneath the earth's surface. Inspired, she considered how these sustainable resources could help reduce dependence on fossil fuels.

During her studies, Mia also came across the fascinating history of **geometry**, which originally helped people measure land and distances. She was amazed at how ancient civilizations used geometric principles to divide territories and build structures that have lasted for centuries.

As Mia became more involved in global issues, she realized that many modern conflicts and decisions were influenced by **geopolitical** factors, such as a country's location, resources, and its access to trade routes. This new perspective sparked a deeper interest in how geography and politics are intertwined in shaping world events.

Mia's love for the earth, its history, and its future grew stronger every day as she pursued her studies, determined to contribute to a better understanding of our planet.

ROOT: "BIO-" (MEANING: "LIFE")

Vocabulary:
The Greek root "bio-" means "life" and is the basis for words that describe living things and the study of life in various forms.

1. **Biology**: The scientific study of living organisms and life processes.

   Example: She majored in **biology** to learn more about plant and animal life.

2. **Biography**: A detailed account of someone's life written by another person.

   Example: The **biography** of the scientist inspired many young readers.

3. **Biome**: A community of plants and animals that occupies a major habitat.

   Example: The rainforest is a richly diverse **biome** teeming with life.

4. **Biodegradable**: Capable of being broken down naturally by microorganisms.

   Example: **Biodegradable** materials help reduce waste in landfills.

5. **Symbiosis**: A close and often long-term interaction between two different organisms, often beneficial.

   Example: In the ocean, clownfish and sea anemones

have a mutual **symbiosis**.

Word Duel: Biodegradable vs. Synthetic

Question: Which word refers to materials that can break down naturally?

   A) Biodegradable
   B) Synthetic

Correct Answer: A) Biodegradable

Explanation: "Biodegradable" refers to materials that decompose through natural processes. "Synthetic" typically describes man-made materials that do not easily break down in nature.

Semantic Scale: Levels of Life Study and Interaction

This scale presents words related to the study of life and how living things interact within ecosystems.

1. **Ecology** – The study of how organisms interact with their environment.

   Example: **Ecology** explores how plants and animals coexist in various habitats.

2. **Biology** – The study of living organisms and life processes.

   Example: **Biology** covers a wide range of topics, from cellular functions to ecosystems.

3. **Botany** – A branch of biology focused on plant life.

   Example: In **botany**, you learn about different species of plants and their habitats.

4. **Zoology** – The scientific study of animals and their behavior.

   Example: **Zoology** includes researching how animals adapt to their environments.

5. **Symbiosis** – A relationship where two different species interact, often beneficially.

   Example: The **symbiosis** between bees and flowers supports pollination.

Language Time Travel: Biology vs. Biography

The term **biology** combines "bio" (life) and "logia" (study of), meaning "the study of life." **Biography** combines "bio" with "graphia" (writing), meaning "writing about life." Over time, biology developed as a scientific discipline studying life in all its forms, while biography became focused on documenting individual lives and their stories.

The Biologist's Discovery:

In her **biology** research, Dr. Harris uncovered a unique **symbiosis** between tree roots and certain fungi, which allowed both to thrive. This finding had exciting implications for understanding **biomes** and how ecosystems function. Inspired by her work, a young writer even composed a **biography** of her, capturing Dr. Harris's dedication to preserving life and promoting the use of **biodegradable** products to protect natural habitats.

ROOT: "PHON-" (MEANING: "SOUND" OR "VOICE")

Vocabulary:

The Greek root "phon-" means "sound" or "voice" and appears in words that relate to auditory elements, speech, and acoustics.

1. **Phonetic**: Relating to sounds of speech; representing sounds with symbols.

    Example: English spelling doesn't always match its <u>phonetic</u> pronunciation.

2. **Cacophony**: A harsh, jarring mixture of sounds.

    Example: The construction site was filled with a <u>cacophony</u> of drills and hammers.

3. **Euphony**: A pleasing, harmonious sound.

    Example: The <u>euphony</u> of the choir's voices filled the cathedral.

4. **Symphony**: A lengthy, complex piece of musical composition, often for an orchestra.

    Example: The orchestra played a Beethoven <u>symphony</u> to a captivated audience.

5. **Megaphone**: A device used to amplify sound and project the voice.

    Example: The coach used a <u>megaphone</u> to give instructions to the players on the field.

Word Duel: Cacophony vs. Euphony

Question: Which word best describes a harsh or jarring combination of sounds?
   A) Cacophony
   B) Euphony

Correct Answer: A) Cacophony

Explanation: "Cacophony" refers to a loud and unpleasant mixture of sounds, often discordant, whereas "euphony" describes sounds that are pleasing and harmonious.

Semantic Scale: Levels of Sound Quality

This scale ranges from harsh, unpleasant sounds to harmonious, beautiful sounds.

1. **Clamor** – A loud, persistent noise, usually from a crowd or protest.

   Example: The **clamor** of the city was overwhelming.

2. **Cacophony** – A mixture of harsh, jarring sounds.

   Example: The **cacophony** of horns and sirens filled the street.

3. **Resonance** – A sound that is deep, full, and reverberates.

   Example: His voice had a **resonance** that captivated everyone.

4. **Euphony** – Pleasant, harmonious sound.

   Example: Her song had a gentle **euphony** that soothed the listeners.

5. **Harmony** – A combination of musical notes that sound pleasing together.

   Example: The **harmony** of voices made the choir's performance unforgettable.

Language Time Travel: Symphony vs. Megaphone

Symphony comes from the Greek "symphonia," meaning "agreement or concord of sound," and eventually evolved to describe musical compositions of harmonious sounds. **Megaphone** combines "mega" (large) with "phon" (sound), originally intended as a device to project sound to large groups.

The Sounds of the City:

The city was filled with the **cacophony** of traffic, people talking, and music playing from shops. In the evening, though, a busker's guitar created a **euphony** that offered a brief escape. Nearby, a street musician played an entire **symphony** on his violin, his music amplified slightly by a simple **megaphone**. The **resonance** of each note echoed down the busy avenue, giving a sense of calm amid the urban clamor.

ROOT: "DICT-" (MEANING: "SPEAK" OR "SAY")

Vocabulary:
The Latin root "dict-" means "to speak" or "to say" and is used in words that involve speaking, declaring, or expressing something.

1. **Dictate**: To say or read aloud something to be written down; to give orders.

    Example: The teacher <u>dictated</u> instructions to the class.

2. **Verdict**: A decision or judgment, often used in a legal context.

    Example: The jury reached a <u>verdict</u> after hours of deliberation.

3. **Predict**: To say or estimate that something will happen in the future.

    Example: Meteorologists <u>predict</u> rain based on weather patterns.

4. **Diction**: The choice and use of words in speech or writing.

    Example: Her clear diction made her presentation easy to understand.

5. **Contradict**: To say the opposite of something someone else has said; to deny.

    Example: He didn't mean to <u>contradict</u> his friend, but he had a different perspective.

Word Duel: Diction vs. Dictate
Question: Which word best describes the choice of words and clarity in speech or writing?
   A) Diction
   B) Dictate
Correct Answer: A) Diction
Explanation: "Diction" refers to the choice of words and clarity in speech or writing, while "dictate" means to give orders or read something aloud for transcription.

Semantic Scale: Levels of Speaking and Expression
This scale presents words that describe types of speech, from making predictions to commanding orders.
   1. **Predict** – To state what will likely happen in the future.
   Example: Economists **predict** changes in the market.
   2. **Declare** – To announce something publicly or formally.
   Example: She **declared** her candidacy for office.
   3. **Dictate** – To speak aloud for transcription or give authoritative orders.
   Example: He **dictated** his message to his assistant.
   4. **Assert** – To state firmly and confidently.
   Example: She **asserted** her opinion during the debate.
   5. **Proclaim** – To make a public announcement or statement, often with emphasis.
   Example: The leader **proclaimed** a new era of peace.

Language Time Travel: Predict vs. Verdict
Predict combines the Latin roots "pre-" (before) and "dict" (say), meaning to say something ahead of time. **Verdict** joins "ver-" (true) with "dict," originally meaning a statement of truth in judgment.

A Judge's Wisdom:
   The judge listened to each witness, careful not to **contradict** any statements too soon. Once all evidence

was heard, she announced the **verdict** with calm **diction**, explaining each part clearly. She then **proclaimed** her support for justice and transparency in the legal process. Her thoughtful words reflected her dedication to fairness, leaving an impact on all who attended the trial.

ROOT: "JECT-" (MEANING: "THROW")

Vocabulary:

The Latin root "ject-" means "to throw" and is used in words that involve the action of casting, projecting, or rejecting something.

1. **Eject**: To throw out or expel something, often forcefully.

   Example: The DVD player <u>ejects</u> the disc with the press of a button.

2. **Inject**: To introduce something, usually a fluid, into something else.

   Example: Doctors <u>inject</u> vaccines to help prevent diseases.

3. **Project**: To throw forward; can mean to display something on a surface or to plan for the future.

   Example: The teacher <u>projected</u> the image onto the screen.

4. **Reject**: To refuse to accept or consider.

   Example: She decided to <u>reject</u> the job offer because it didn't match her career goals.

5. **Trajectory**: The path followed by an object thrown or projected into space.

   Example: The <u>trajectory</u> of the rocket was carefully calculated by scientists.

Word Duel: Eject vs. Inject
Question: Which word best describes introducing a substance into something else?
   A) Eject
   B) Inject
Correct Answer: B) Inject
Explanation: "Inject" means to introduce something, usually a fluid, into something else, while "eject" means to throw something out or expel it.

Semantic Scale: Levels of Throwing and Casting
This scale presents words that describe actions of throwing, casting, or rejecting from mild to strong.
   1. **Toss** – To throw something lightly or casually.
   Example: He **tossed** his keys onto the table.
   2. **Propel** – To drive or push forward.
   Example: The engine **propels** the boat through the water.
   3. **Project** – To cast forward, or to display something outward.
   Example: The stage lights **project** patterns across the auditorium.
   4. **Launch** – To send forcefully into motion, often into air or space.
   Example: The company is ready to **launch** its new product next month.
   5. **Catapult** – To throw or launch with great force, often suddenly.
   Example: The roller coaster **catapulted** riders through twists and loops.

Language Time Travel: Trajectory vs. Project
Trajectory originates from the Latin "trajectoria," meaning "a throwing across," and is used in modern contexts to describe the path of an object in motion. **Project** combines "pro-" (forward) with "ject" (throw) and originally meant to "throw forward," but has evolved to also mean planning for the

future.

The Launch of the Space Mission:

Engineers carefully calculated the rocket's **trajectory** to ensure a safe journey. As the engines ignited, the vehicle **catapulted** into space, and the crowd watched as it quickly **projected** into the sky. The rocket continued to **propel** forward, following its path with precision, reaching speeds that would eventually **eject** the cargo into orbit. The launch was a success, a remarkable feat that would inspire future **projects** in space exploration.

ROOT: "VIV-" (MEANING: "LIFE")

Vocabulary:

The Latin root "viv-" refers to life, living, or the act of being alive, and appears in words related to living organisms or vitality.

1. **Vivid**: Having strong, clear, and lively appearance or character.

    Example: The artist used vivid colors to bring the landscape to life.

2. **Revive**: To bring something back to life or consciousness.

    Example: The paramedics worked quickly to revive the patient after the accident.

3. **Vivacious**: Full of life and energy, typically used to describe a person.

    Example: Her vivacious personality made her the life of every party.

4. **Survive**: To continue to live or exist, especially after a difficult or dangerous situation.

    Example: The explorers managed to survive the harsh winter in the mountains.

5. **Vivarium**: An enclosure for keeping live animals under controlled conditions.

    Example: The scientist studied amphibians in a large vivarium at the research facility.

Word Duel: Vivacious vs. Revive
Question: Which word best describes someone full of energy and life?
   A) Vivacious
   B) Revive
Correct Answer: A) Vivacious
Explanation: "Vivacious" describes a person full of life and energy, while "revive" refers to bringing something back to life or reawakening.

Semantic Scale: Levels of Vitality
This scale goes from a state of being full of life to barely surviving.
   1. **Lively** – Energetic and full of spirit.
   Example: The crowd was **lively**, dancing and singing throughout the concert.
   2. **Vivacious** – Full of enthusiasm and high-spirited energy.
   Example: The **vivacious** woman entertained everyone with her humor.
   3. **Vivid** – Clear and intense, bringing things to life in one's imagination.
   Example: The movie had **vivid** special effects that made the battle scenes unforgettable.
   4. **Survive** – To continue living or existing despite hardship.
   Example: They managed to **survive** the dangerous storm without major injuries.
   5. **Revive** – To restore or bring back to life, often used metaphorically for something that was almost lost.
   Example: The chef worked hard to **revive** the restaurant's old menu items.

Language Time Travel: Survive vs. Vivid
"Survive" comes from the Latin "sub" (under) and "vivere" (to live), meaning to live through or outlast something. **Vivid** comes from the Latin "vivus" (alive), describing something as

full of life or appearing as if it's alive.

The Revitalized Town:

After the devastating storm, the small town seemed lifeless, but a group of determined residents worked tirelessly to **revive** it. They planted new trees, repaired homes, and restored businesses. The mayor, known for her **vivacious** spirit, led the effort, inspiring everyone with her energy. As the town came back to life, it became a **vivid** example of resilience. The town's revival was a testament to the strength of the community, proving that with enough determination, they could **survive** anything.

ROOT: "DUC-" (MEANING: "LEAD")

Vocabulary:

The Latin root "duc-" comes from "ducere," meaning "to lead" or "to guide." This root appears in words that involve leadership, guidance, or direction.

1. **Introduce**: To bring something or someone into a new environment or group; to lead in.

   Example: The professor will <u>introduce</u> the guest speaker at the seminar.

2. **Conduct**: To lead or guide something, often used for activities or behavior.

   Example: The orchestra conductor <u>conducted</u> the performance flawlessly.

3. **Produce**: To create or bring forth; to lead something into existence.

   Example: The company plans to <u>produce</u> a new line of smartphones.

4. **Abduct**: To take someone away by force or threat; to lead away illegally.

   Example: The police are investigating the case of a child who was <u>abducted</u> from the park.

5. **Induce**: To lead someone to do something, especially through persuasion or influence.

   Example: The advertisement may <u>induce</u> customers to

buy more products.

Word Duel: Produce vs. Abduct

Question: Which word best describes leading someone away by force or deception?

    A) Produce
    B) Abduct

Correct Answer: B) Abduct

Explanation: "Abduct" means to take someone away by force, while "produce" means to create or bring something into existence.

Semantic Scale: Levels of Leading

This scale explores actions related to leading, from introducing to more forceful directions.

1. **Introduce** – To bring something new into a group or place.

Example: She was the first to **introduce** the new product at the conference.

2. **Induce** – To lead someone toward a specific action or behavior, often through influence.

Example: The weather might **induce** people to stay indoors.

3. **Conduct** – To direct or guide something, often in a formal manner.

Example: He was hired to **conduct** the research study.

4. **Produce** – To bring something into existence, especially a product or outcome.

Example: The team will **produce** a report by the end of the month.

5. **Abduct** – To lead someone away forcibly or by deception.

Example: The criminal was caught attempting to **abduct** the child.

Language Time Travel: Produce vs. Induce

"Produce" comes from the Latin "producere" (to bring forward), meaning to make or bring something into existence.

Induce comes from "inducere" (to lead into), which refers to leading someone into a particular course of action or state.

The Leadership Challenge:

In the village, the community leader had to **conduct** the planning meetings to rebuild after the disaster. She worked hard to **introduce** new ideas for growth and to **produce** a detailed plan for recovery. Her speeches would often **induce** others to contribute their time and resources, and her persuasive abilities were unparalleled. However, not everyone agreed with her approach, and a group tried to **abduct** the plan for their own interests. But through strong leadership, she was able to lead the team back to her original vision.

ROOT: "SPECT-" (MEANING: "LOOK" OR "SEE")

Vocabulary:

The Latin root "spect-" comes from "specere," meaning "to look" or "to see." This root appears in words related to viewing, observing, or seeing.

1. **Spectacle**: A visually striking performance or display, often impressive or unusual.

    Example: The fireworks display was a stunning <u>spectacle</u> that lit up the night sky.

2. **Inspect**: To look at something closely, often for the purpose of checking or examining.

    Example: The mechanic will <u>inspect</u> the car to make sure everything is working properly.

3. **Prospect**: The outlook or expectation for the future, or a potential opportunity.

    Example: The job <u>prospects</u> in the new city are promising for skilled workers.

4. **Aspect**: A particular part or feature of something; a way in which something can be viewed.

    Example: One <u>aspect</u> of the new policy is its impact on the environment.

5. **Retrospective**: Looking back on or dealing with past events or situations.

    Example: The museum held a <u>retrospective</u> exhibit

showcasing the artist's entire career.

Word Duel: Spectacle vs. Inspect

Question: Which word best describes a careful examination or observation of something?

A) Spectacle
B) Inspect

Correct Answer: B) Inspect

Explanation: "Inspect" refers to closely looking at something to check or examine it, while "spectacle" refers to a visually striking event or performance.

Types of Observation

This list moves from general viewing to more detailed or reflective observation.

1. **Spectacle** – A visually impressive event.

    Example: The **spectacle** of the parade filled the streets with excitement.

2. **Aspect** – A specific feature or part of something that can be viewed or considered.

    Example: One **aspect** of the novel was its intricate plot twists.

3. **Prospect** – The expected or anticipated outcome or opportunity, often seen as future possibilities.

    Example: The **prospects** for the new tech company are optimistic.

4. **Inspect** – To examine something carefully.

    Example: She asked the technician to **inspect** the wiring for any issues.

5. **Retrospective** – Looking back on past events with reflection or review.

    Example: The documentary provided a **retrospective** view of the city's growth over the decades.

Language Time Travel: Prospect vs. Retrospective

"Prospect" comes from the Latin "prospectus" (view or outlook), referring to the future or what is expected. **Retrospective** comes from "retro" (back) and "specere" (to look), meaning looking back on or reflecting on past events.

The Spectacular Journey:

The expedition team set off on a thrilling journey to explore an ancient temple. As they approached the entrance, the sight of the towering stone walls was a **spectacle**, capturing the awe of every member. They stopped to **inspect** the carvings along the walls, fascinated by their age and detail. Looking around, one team member considered the **prospects** of finding more hidden chambers, while another took a more reflective view of the journey in a **retrospective** manner. Each moment of the journey offered a new **aspect** of discovery, but the temple's grand entrance would forever be the most memorable **spectacle** they had witnessed.

ROOT: - "VERT-" (MEANING: "TURN")

Vocabulary:

The Latin root "vert-" comes from "vertere," meaning "to turn." This root is seen in words related to turning, changing direction, or altering something.

1. **Convert**: To change or transform something into a different form or use.

    Example: She decided to **convert** the spare room into an art studio.

2. **Invert**: To reverse or turn something upside down.

    Example: The magician will **invert** the glass to make the coin disappear.

3. **Revert**: To return to a previous state or condition.

    Example: After the trial period, the system will **revert** to its original settings.

4. **Extrovert**: A person who is outgoing, sociable, and focuses on the external world.

    Example: She is an **extrovert** who loves attending social gatherings and making new friends.

5. **Subvert**: To undermine or overthrow something, especially an established system or authority.

    Example: The group attempted to **subvert** the government's policies through protests.

Word Duel: Convert vs. Revert

Question: Which word describes changing something into a different form or use?
    A) Convert
    B) Revert
Correct Answer: A) Convert
Explanation: "Convert" refers to changing something into a different form or use, while "revert" means returning to a previous state or condition.

Semantic Scale: Levels of Change
This scale shows words related to change or turning, from transforming to reversing.

    1. **Convert** – To change something into a different form or use.
    Example: The building was **converted** into a museum.
    2. **Invert** – To turn something upside down or reverse its position.
    Example: He had to **invert** the cup to check for any hidden objects.
    3. **Revert** – To return to a previous state or condition.
    Example: After the test, the settings will **revert** to their original state.
    4. **Subvert** – To undermine or challenge an established system.
    Example: The activists worked to **subvert** the old system of government.
    5. **Extrovert** – A person who is outgoing and enjoys interacting with others.
    Example: As an **extrovert**, she enjoys meeting new people at every event.

Language Time Travel: Extrovert vs. Introvert
"Extrovert" comes from the Latin "extra" (outside) and "vertere" (to turn), meaning someone who turns their focus outward. **Introvert**, on the other hand, comes from "intro" (inward), describing someone who turns their focus inwardly, preferring solitude or small groups.

The Turning Point:

In a small village, two friends, Alice and Ben, were known for their contrasting personalities. Alice was an **extrovert**, always engaging with the community and making new connections. Ben, however, preferred a more quiet lifestyle and often found himself wishing to **revert** to his old, solitary ways. One day, Ben decided to **convert** his spare room into a small library to enjoy his solitude in a more peaceful space. Alice, eager to help, invited him to an event at the community center. Ben felt a bit out of place but didn't want to **invert** his decision to attend. Afterward, Alice explained how her social nature helped her **subvert** feelings of isolation, suggesting that a balance between both approaches could lead to a fulfilling life.

ROOT: "FORM-" (MEANING: "SHAPE" OR "FORM")

Vocabulary:
The Latin root "form-" comes from "forma," meaning "shape" or "appearance." It appears in words related to shaping, molding, or the structure of something.

1. **Formulate:** To create or devise something, often with careful planning or arrangement.

Example: The company will <u>formulate</u> a new marketing strategy for the upcoming year.

2. **Transform:** To change in form, appearance, or structure.

Example: The old factory was <u>transformed</u> into a modern art gallery.

3. **Conform:** To comply with established standards or rules, or to make something match.

Example: The new employee had to conform to the company's strict dress code.

4. **Reform:** To make changes in order to improve something, typically in a social or political context.

Example: The government decided to <u>reform</u> the healthcare system to provide better access to care.

5. **Inform:** To give someone knowledge or information.

Example: She will <u>inform</u> the team about the changes in the project timeline.

Word Duel: Transform vs. Conform
Question: Which word describes changing something in a significant way, often for the better?
    A) Transform
    B) Conform
Correct Answer: A) Transform
Explanation: "Transform" refers to changing something significantly, while "conform" means to comply or fit into an existing structure, typically without making changes.

Degrees of Shaping and Changing
This list explores words related to shaping, from changing the form of something to adhering to existing forms.
    1. **Formulate** – To create or develop a plan or idea.
Example: He took weeks to **formulate** the perfect proposal.
    2. **Reform** – To make improvements or changes to improve something.
Example: They wanted to **reform** the law to make it more equitable.
    3. **Transform** – To undergo a significant change, often for the better.
Example: The town has been **transformed** by new development projects.
    4. **Conform** – To follow rules or adapt to a particular set of standards.
Example: The children were expected to **conform** to the classroom rules.
    5. **Inform** – To provide someone with important knowledge or news.
Example: The teacher will **inform** the class about the upcoming exam.

Language Time Travel: Formulate vs. Inform
The word "formulate" comes from the Latin "formulatus," meaning "to shape or create a form." It evolved into the idea of devising plans or systems. On the other hand, "inform"

comes from "informare," meaning "to give shape to the mind" or "to educate." So while "formulate" focuses on shaping ideas, "inform" is more about passing knowledge.

The Transformative Power of Change:

In a town plagued by inefficiency, the local council began to reform its outdated laws. Citizens were encouraged to conform to new guidelines that promised fairness and equality. At the same time, a new project was launched to transform the city's infrastructure, turning old, abandoned buildings into modern apartments. As they gathered to discuss the changes, the mayor sought to inform the residents about how these developments would benefit the community. Meanwhile, an advisor was hired to formulate a strategy to ensure that the transformation would proceed smoothly, helping the town reach its full potential.

ROOT: "VERS-" (MEANING: "TURN")

Vocabulary:
The root **"vers-"** comes from the Latin word "vertere," meaning "to turn" or "to change direction." It appears in words that involve turning, changing, or reversing a state or position.

1. **Convert** – To change something into a different form, state, or use.

    Example: She decided to convert her spare room into a home office.

2. **Revert** – To return to a previous state or condition.

    Example: After the software update, the settings will revert to their default values.

3. **Versatile** – Able to adapt or be used for many different purposes.

    Example: The new kitchen tool is highly versatile, functioning as a blender, mixer, and food processor.

4. **Inversion** – The action of turning something upside down or reversing its position or order.

    Example: The magician's trick involved an inversion of the deck of cards, causing them to appear in a completely different order.

Word Duel: Convert vs. Revert
Question: Which word describes returning something to a previous state or condition?

A) Convert
B) Revert

Correct Answer: B) Revert

Explanation: "Convert" refers to changing something into a new form or state, while "revert" means to return to a previous form or condition.

Semantic Scale: Levels of Changing and Turning

This scale explores words related to turning or changing, from small adaptations to complete reversals.

1. **Versatile** – Capable of adapting to various functions or roles.

   Example: The actor's **versatile** talents allowed him to play a wide range of characters.

2. **Convert** – To change into a different form or state.

   Example: He chose to **convert** to a plant-based diet for health reasons.

3. **Inversion** – A complete reversal or turning upside down.

   Example: The **inversion** of the traditional story structure made the film feel fresh and innovative.

4. **Revert** – To return to a previous state or condition.

   Example: The website's design will **revert** back to its original layout after a few tweaks.

Language Time Travel: Convert vs. Versatile

The word **convert** comes from the Latin "convertere," meaning "to turn around" or "to change." It is used for changes in form, beliefs, or actions. **Versatile**, on the other hand, comes from the Latin "versatilis," meaning "apt to turn or change," and refers to something or someone able to perform many different tasks or take on various roles.

The Turning of Ideas and States:

Marcus was known for his **versatile** abilities. As a photographer, he could **convert** any ordinary scene into something extraordinary with just a few adjustments. One day, during a photoshoot, the weather took an unexpected turn, forcing Marcus to **revert** to his backup plan. After a few adjustments, he performed an **inversion** of his original concept, resulting in a creative, unexpected outcome. His ability to turn challenges into opportunities made him a successful and sought-after professional in his field.

ROOT: "GRAD-" (MEANING: "STEP" OR "DEGREE")

Vocabulary:
The root **"grad-"** comes from the Latin word "gradus," meaning "step" or "degree." It is found in words related to steps, levels, or progression, whether physical, intellectual, or social.

1. **Graduate** – To complete a level of education, often from a school or university.

Example: After four years of hard work, she was proud to graduate with honors from college.

2. **Gradual** – Happening slowly or in small steps over time.

Example: There was a gradual change in the weather, with temperatures rising each day.

3. **Progress** – Forward movement or development towards a goal or better condition.

Example: The team showed significant progress after months of practice and strategy sessions.

4. **Degrade** – To lower in rank, status, or quality; to treat someone with disrespect.

Example: The manager's harsh comments were meant to degrade the employee's self-esteem.

Word Duel: Graduate vs. Degrade
Question: Which word refers to improving or advancing in level or status?

A) Graduate
B) Degrade

Correct Answer: A) Graduate

Explanation: "Graduate" refers to advancing or moving to a higher level, typically in education. "Degrade," on the other hand, means to lower or diminish in quality or status.

Levels of Advancement and Decline

This list explores words related to moving forward (progress) and moving backward or being reduced (degrade), from slow changes to significant alterations.

1. **Gradual** – Occurring in small, often barely noticeable steps.

    Example: The transition to the new management style was **gradual**, allowing employees time to adjust.

2. **Progress** – Advancement or movement toward a more developed or improved state.

    Example: The community made great **progress** in improving local healthcare services.

3. **Graduate** – To move up to the next level or step, often referring to education.

    Example: After graduating, she planned to pursue a career in research.

4. **Degrade** – To lower in rank, dignity, or quality.

    Example: The mistreatment of workers served to **degrade** the company's reputation.

Language Time Travel: Graduate vs. Gradual

"Graduate" comes from the Latin "gradus," meaning "step," and originally referred to moving from one step to the next, especially in education. "Gradual" comes from the same root but evolved to describe something happening in slow, small steps over time, without the need for a sudden transition.

The Steps of Life:

John, a student, worked hard to **graduate** with a degree in engineering. He had made **gradual** progress through his studies, slowly building up his skills and knowledge over time.

After graduation, he joined a company that valued innovation and progress. However, when a new manager started, his leadership style seemed to **degrade** the team's morale, creating tension in the workplace. John, who believed in steady progress, took the initiative to improve the team's situation by suggesting a **gradual** approach to change, just as he had done with his education.

ROOT: "CRED-" (MEANING: "BELIEVE" OR "TRUST")

Vocabulary:

The root **"cred-"** comes from the Latin word "credere," meaning "to believe" or "to trust." It appears in words related to belief, trustworthiness, and credibility.

1. **Credible** – Believable or trustworthy; able to be trusted or relied upon.

   Example: The witness's testimony was <u>credible</u>, and the jury believed his version of events.

2. **Incredible** – So extraordinary that it is hard to believe; unbelievable.

   Example: The magician's performance was so amazing that it seemed <u>incredible</u>.

3. **Credit** – Trust or belief in someone's ability or the acknowledgment of their work or contributions.

   Example: She received <u>credit</u> for her role in the successful project.

4. **Credential** – A qualification or achievement that proves a person's ability or trustworthiness.

   Example: His impressive <u>credentials</u> earned him a position as the lead scientist at the company.

Word Duel: Credible vs. Incredible

Question: Which word describes something that is believable or trustworthy?
   A) Credible
   B) Incredible

Correct Answer: A) Credible

Explanation: "Credible" refers to something or someone that can be trusted or believed. "Incredible," however, describes something that is so extraordinary or unbelievable that it's hard to trust or believe.

Semantic Scale: Levels of Belief and Trustworthiness

This scale shows words related to belief and trust, ranging from believable to something that is hard to trust.

1. **Credential** – Something that proves trustworthiness or ability.

    Example: The professor showed his **credentials** before starting his lecture.

2. **Credible** – Believable or trustworthy.

    Example: His report was **credible** because it was based on reliable sources.

3. **Credit** – Recognition or acknowledgment of someone's efforts.

    Example: The actor received **credit** for his exceptional performance in the film.

4. **Incredible** – So extraordinary that it is difficult to believe.

    Example: The athlete's **incredible** achievement of breaking three world records in one year stunned everyone.

Language Time Travel: Credible vs. Incredible

Both **credible** and **incredible** share the same root "cred-" from the Latin "credere" (to believe). **Credible** refers to something that is believable or trustworthy, while **incredible** adds a negative prefix "in-" to imply that it is too extraordinary to be believed or trusted easily.

The Importance of Trust:

Sarah was a **credible** expert in her field of cybersecurity, known for her vast knowledge and integrity. Her **credentials** were impeccable, making her an ideal candidate for a prestigious research position. One day, Sarah heard an **incredible** story about a new breakthrough in artificial intelligence. At first, she was skeptical, as it seemed too extraordinary to be true. However, after doing her research and finding supporting evidence, she gave the new theory the **credit** it deserved, sharing her findings with the academic community.

ROOT: "MIT-" OR "MISS-" (MEANING: "SEND")

Vocabulary:

The roots **"mit-"** and **"miss-"** come from the Latin word "mittere," meaning "to send." These roots appear in words related to sending or dispatching something, either physically, emotionally, or metaphorically.

1. **Emit** – To send out, release, or give off (something, like light, sound, or gas).

   Example: The factory chimney began to **emit** thick smoke, signaling a malfunction.

2. **Transmit** – To send something from one person, place, or thing to another.

   Example: The technician worked to **transmit** the data from the old server to the new one.

3. **Mission** – A task or duty to be accomplished, often with a sense of purpose or responsibility.

   Example: The astronauts embarked on a space **mission** to repair the satellite.

4. **Dismiss** – To send away or allow someone to leave; also, to disregard or reject something as unimportant.

   Example: The teacher chose to **dismiss** the students early for the holiday break.

Word Duel: Emit vs. Dismiss

Question: Which word refers to sending something away or allowing someone to leave?
   A) Emit
   B) Dismiss

Correct Answer: B) Dismiss

Explanation: "Emit" refers to sending something out, like light or sound, while "dismiss" refers to sending someone away, usually from a place or activity.

Language Time Travel: Emit vs. Mission

The word **emit** comes from the Latin "emittere," meaning "to send out." It originally referred to sending or giving off something, such as light or heat. **Mission**, on the other hand, comes from the Latin "missio," meaning "sending" or "dispatch." Historically, it referred to sending people on important tasks or purposes, especially in a religious or diplomatic context.

Sending Messages and Tasks:

Anna had always been fascinated by space exploration. When she was selected for a critical **mission** to research potential life on Mars, she felt honored. She had to **transmit** data back to Earth every day, documenting any findings she made. One evening, as she worked late into the night, her computer began to **emit** a strange buzzing sound, signaling a system error. Anna calmly fixed the issue, but before long, she was **dismissed** from the mission team for not reporting the malfunction immediately, though she later proved her actions were justified.

ROOT: "CIDE-" (MEANING: "KILL" OR "CUT")

Vocabulary:
The root **"cide-"** comes from the Latin word "caedere," meaning "to kill" or "to cut." This root appears in words that refer to killing, destruction, or cutting down, whether literally or figuratively.

1. **Homicide** – The act of killing another person.

   Example: The detective was assigned to investigate the **homicide** that occurred late last night.

2. **Pesticide** – A chemical substance used to kill pests or unwanted organisms.

   Example: The farmer sprayed **pesticide** on the crops to protect them from insects.

3. **Genocide** – The deliberate killing of a large number of people, particularly a particular ethnic group or nation.

   Example: The country was condemned internationally for its involvement in the **genocide** that took place during the war.

4. **Suicidal** – Relating to or having tendencies toward self-harm or killing oneself.

   Example: After hearing the tragic news, he started to feel **suicidal**, but he sought help immediately.

Word Duel: Homicide vs. Genocide

Question: Which word refers to the mass killing of a specific ethnic group or population?
A) Homicide
B) Genocide

Correct Answer: B) Genocide

Explanation: "Homicide" refers to the killing of one person, while "genocide" refers to the deliberate and systematic killing of a large group of people, often based on race, religion, or ethnicity.

Semantic Scale: Levels of Killing or Destruction

This scale explores words related to killing or cutting, from individual acts to large-scale destruction.

1. **Suicidal** – The tendency or act of killing oneself.
Example: He was feeling **suicidal** after the breakdown in his personal life but reached out for support.

2. **Homicide** – The killing of another person.
Example: The detective worked tirelessly on the **homicide** case, seeking justice for the victim.

3. **Pesticide** – A substance used to kill unwanted organisms, typically pests or insects.
Example: The use of **pesticide** was necessary to prevent the crops from being destroyed by the insects.

4. **Genocide** – The systematic killing of a particular group, often for political or ideological reasons.
Example: The historical records revealed the horrific acts of **genocide** that affected millions.

Language Time Travel: Homicide vs. Pesticide

Both words come from the Latin root "caedere" (to cut or kill). **Homicide** comes from "homo" (human), meaning the killing of a person. **Pesticide** comes from "pestis" (pest or plague), referring to substances that kill pests. Over time, these terms have expanded to describe various forms of killing or elimination, either human-related or in agriculture.

The Tragic Consequences:

During a difficult period of unrest, many families faced the horrors of **genocide**, losing loved ones to systematic violence and hatred. In one case, a witness was devastated when her father was a victim of **homicide**—a senseless killing that could have been prevented. As the community struggled to find justice, the local government implemented measures to deal with **pesticides** harming the environment, though this was a minor issue compared to the ongoing crisis. Meanwhile, a young man, feeling **suicidal** after losing everything, found the courage to speak out, ultimately becoming an advocate for peace and justice.

ROOT: "CIRCUM-" (MEANING : "AROUND")

Vocabulary:

The root **"circum-"** comes from the Latin word "circum," meaning "around." This root appears in words that refer to things surrounding, encircling, or going around something, either physically or metaphorically.

1. **Circumference** – The distance around the edge of a circle or round object.
   - *Example*: The **circumference** of the Earth is about 40,075 kilometers.
2. **Circumvent** – To find a way around or bypass something, often in a clever or deceitful way.
   - *Example*: The hackers tried to **circumvent** the security system by exploiting a loophole.
3. **Circumstantial** – Related to or depending on the circumstances; often used to describe indirect or secondary evidence.
   - *Example*: The detective could not make an arrest based on the **circumstantial** evidence alone.
4. **Circumlocution** – The use of many words to express something that could be said more simply; talking around an issue.
   - *Example*: Instead of answering directly, he

used **circumlocution** to avoid giving a clear response.

Word Duel: Circumference vs. Circumlocution

Question: Which word refers to the distance around something, typically a circle?

    A) Circumference
    B) Circumlocution

Correct Answer: A) Circumference

Explanation: "Circumference" refers to the measurement around the edge of a circle, while "circumlocution" refers to the act of using many words to avoid a direct answer or to describe something indirectly.

Surrounding or Going Around

This list explores words related to "around" or "circling," from geometric measurements to indirect ways of addressing topics.

1. **Circumference** – The measurement around a circular object or boundary.
    - *Example*: The **circumference** of the park's walking track was over two miles.
2. **Circumlocution** – Speaking in a roundabout way, using more words than necessary.
    - *Example*: His response was full of **circumlocution**, making it hard to understand his true point.
3. **Circumstantial** – Referring to conditions or factors that depend on the specific situation or context.
    - *Example*: The lawyer's argument was based on **circumstantial** details rather than direct evidence.
4. **Circumvent** – To cleverly avoid something, often bypassing rules or obstacles.
    - *Example*: They managed to **circumvent** the law by finding a loophole in the regulations.

Language Time Travel: Circumference vs. Circumvent

Both **circumference** and **circumvent** share the Latin root **"circum-"**, meaning "around." **Circumference** comes from "ferre" (to carry), referring to the distance around a circle, as if carrying a measurement around. **Circumvent**, on the other hand, uses the Latin verb "venire" (to come), meaning to go around or outwit something, usually to avoid an obstacle.

Around the Issue:

During the exploration of the ancient city, the archaeologist measured the **circumference** of a massive stone circle that was believed to be part of a ritualistic site. As they examined the area, they encountered a legal challenge; a law prevented them from digging further. However, they found a way to **circumvent** the regulation by applying for an exemption, arguing that the discovery was of historical significance. Meanwhile, a journalist tried to cover the story but resorted to **circumlocution**, avoiding direct questions and instead providing vague statements. The evidence for their claims remained **circumstantial**, lacking clear proof but compelling enough to spark public interest.

ROOT: "TEMPOR-" (MEANING: "TIME")

Vocabulary:
The root **"tempor-"** is derived from the Latin word **"tempus,"** meaning time. It appears in words related to time, its passage, and how time is measured or experienced.

1. **Temporary**: Lasting for a limited time.
   - *Example*: The museum is offering a **temporary** exhibit on ancient art.
2. **Contemporary**: Existing or occurring at the same time.
   - *Example*: His art is often compared to that of other **contemporary** painters.
3. **Tempo**: The speed or rate at which something happens, especially in music.
   - *Example*: The **tempo** of the song picked up as it reached the chorus.
4. **Temporal**: Relating to time or the physical world.
   - *Example*: He focused on the **temporal** concerns of daily life, ignoring the deeper spiritual questions.

Word Duel: Temporary vs. Permanent
Question: Which word refers to something that is meant to last for a limited period of time?
   A.) Temporary

B.) Permanent

Correct Answer: Temporary

Explanation: "Temporary" refers to something that is not meant to last forever, while "permanent" refers to something lasting indefinitely.

Semantic Scale: Duration of Time

This scale shows words relating to different lengths of time:

1. **Momentary**: Lasting for just a moment.
   Example: His **momentary** hesitation caused him to miss the opportunity.
2. **Short-term**: Brief in duration.
   Example: They are working on a **short-term** project for the next month.
3. **Temporary**: Meant to last for a limited time.
   Example: The store will be closed for **temporary** renovations.
4. **Long-term**: Extending over a long period.
   Example: She's planning for **long-term** success in her career.
5. **Eternal**: Lasting forever.
   Example: They made an **eternal** vow to remain together.

Story: The Clock of Time

In the village of Hillside, there stood an ancient clock tower that had been there for centuries. It was known as the "Clock of Time" because, unlike most clocks, it didn't race against time. It moved at a peaceful pace, reminding villagers to value each moment, no matter how **temporary**.

One day, a young man named Thomas, used to the rush of city life, came to visit his grandmother. He was always on a tight schedule, constantly rushing through his day. When he saw the slow-moving clock, he asked, "Why is the clock so slow?"

His grandmother smiled and said, "In our village, we don't focus on the passing of time. We embrace it. Time is not just a **temporary** thing to manage. It's something to live in the present with, to cherish each moment as it comes."

Thomas stood before the clock, feeling a shift in his perspective. For the first time, he noticed how the gentle **tempo** of the clock's ticking matched the calm around him. He realized that he had spent so much time rushing that he had forgotten to live.

ROOT: "AGN-" (MEANING: "TO KNOW" OR "RECOGNIZE")

Origin:
The root **"agn-"** comes from the Latin **"agnosco,"** meaning **"to know"** or **"to recognize."** This root appears in words related to knowledge, awareness, or recognition, emphasizing understanding or the lack of it.

Vocabulary:
1. **Agnostic**: A person who believes that the existence of God or the divine is unknown or unknowable.
   Example: She described herself as **agnostic** because she wasn't sure whether a higher power existed.
2. **Ignorant**: Lacking knowledge or awareness in general; uneducated.
   Example: His **ignorant** comments about the topic showed he hadn't done any research.
3. **Recognition**: The identification of something or someone as having been seen before, or acknowledging someone's achievements.
   Example: The company gave him **recognition** for his hard work with an employee of the year award.
4. **Cognition**: The mental action or process of acquiring knowledge and understanding through thought,

experience, and the senses.
Example: **Cognition** is essential in problem-solving and decision-making.

Word Duel: Agnostic vs. Atheist
Question: Which word refers to someone who believes that the existence of God or a higher power is unknown or unknowable?

A.) Agnostic
B.) Atheist

Correct Answer: **Agnostic**
Explanation: An **agnostic** person is unsure about the existence of God or a higher power, while an **atheist** believes that no gods or higher powers exist.

Semantic Scale: Knowledge and Awareness
This scale shows words from a lack of knowledge to deep understanding:

1. **Ignorant**: Lacking knowledge or awareness.
   Example: She was **ignorant** of the cultural practices in the region.
2. **Aware**: Having knowledge of a situation or fact.
   Example: He was **aware** of the changes happening in his company.
3. **Knowledgeable**: Having extensive knowledge.
   Example: The professor was extremely **knowledgeable** about the subject.
4. **Cognitive**: Related to the process of knowing and understanding.
   Example: **Cognitive** development in children is a vital area of study in psychology.
5. **Recognized**: Acknowledged or accepted.
   Example: She was a **recognized** expert in her field of research.
6. **Enlightened**: Having gained profound knowledge or insight.
   Example: His travels through the world made him

more **enlightened** about diverse cultures and beliefs.

Brief Story: The Journey of Understanding

Lara had always been curious about life's big questions but never found solid answers. Raised in a family where people strongly believed in religion, she often wondered whether there was a greater truth. While her friends were **agnostic**, unsure about the existence of a higher power, Lara felt torn between belief and doubt.

One day, after years of questioning, she had a conversation with her grandfather. He had spent his life in search of wisdom and was a well-respected figure in the community. "Grandpa," she asked, "how did you come to understand what's true?"

He smiled and replied, "It's not about having all the **recognition** of the answers. It's about the process of **cognition**—understanding through your experiences and being open to learning."

Lara thought deeply about his words. She realized that understanding, whether about the divine or life itself, came not from certainty, but from the willingness to explore and recognize the unknown. It was the journey of knowledge that mattered, and she began to embrace that.

ROOT: "JUR-" (MEANING: "LAW" OR "RIGHT")

Origin:
The root **"jur-"** comes from the Latin word **"juris,"** meaning **"law"** or **"right."** It is used in words related to legal matters, rights, or the justice system, reflecting authority, legal power, and adherence to rules.

Example Words:
1. **Jury**: A group of people who are selected to give a verdict in a legal case.
   Example: The **jury** deliberated for hours before reaching a decision.
2. **Jurisdiction**: The official power to make legal decisions and judgments.
   Example: The court has **jurisdiction** over all criminal cases in this region.
3. **Perjury**: The act of lying or making false statements under oath.
   Example: The witness was charged with **perjury** after being caught lying during the trial.
4. **Jurisprudence**: The theory or philosophy of law.
   Example: He studied **jurisprudence** to understand the principles behind legal systems.

Word Duel: Jury vs. Jury Rigged
Question: Which term refers to a group of people selected to

decide the outcome of a case in a court of law?
   A.) Jury
   B.) Jury Rigged

Correct Answer: Jury

Explanation: The word **jury** refers to a group of people who assess a case in court. **Jury rigged**, on the other hand, refers to something that has been hastily or temporarily put together, not related to legal matters.

Law and Order

This list shows words related to law, from official legal actions to violations of law:

1. **Jurisdiction**: The area or authority in which legal power is exercised.
   Example: The judge had **jurisdiction** over all civil cases in the county.
2. **Legal**: Pertaining to the law or permissible under the law.
   Example: It is **legal** to drive with a valid driver's license.
3. **Lawful**: Conforming to the law; allowed by law.
   Example: The search was conducted in a **lawful** manner.
4. **Jurisdictional**: Relating to the authority to make legal decisions.
   Example: The court had **jurisdictional** authority over the case.
5. **Perjury**: Lying under oath, a criminal offense.
   Example: **Perjury** is a serious crime in any legal system.
6. **Justice**: The fair and just treatment according to law.
   Example: The victims hoped for **justice** after the trial.

Story: The Trial of Truth

In the town of Larkspur, a crucial trial was taking place. The town's mayor had been accused of **perjury** after being caught lying under oath about a controversial land deal. The courtroom buzzed with tension as the **jury** filed in to hear the case.

The lawyer for the defense argued that the mayor had made an honest mistake, while the prosecution presented compelling evidence that the mayor had intentionally lied. The **jurisdiction** of the court meant that this case could set a precedent for other similar cases in the region.

As the trial progressed, the judge reminded everyone that **jurisprudence** required that the law be applied fairly, regardless of who was involved. The **jury** deliberated for hours, and after much discussion, they returned with their verdict. The mayor was found guilty of **perjury**.

The case had shown the importance of upholding **jurisprudence**, ensuring that justice was done, and that even those in power must abide by the law. It was a reminder that in the eyes of the law, everyone's **rights** were equal, and justice would prevail.

ROOT: "CLAM-" (MEANING: "SHOUT" OR "CRY OUT")

Origin:
The root **"clam-"** comes from the Latin **"clamare,"** meaning **"to shout"** or **"to cry out."** It appears in words related to calling out, loud expressions, or public declarations, reflecting an action of speaking out loudly or making something known.

Vocabulary:
- **Clamor**: A loud and persistent outcry, often from a group of people.
  Example: The **clamor** of the crowd grew louder as they awaited the announcement.
- **Exclaim**: To cry out suddenly, often with strong emotion.
  Example: "I can't believe it!" she **exclaimed** after hearing the good news.
- **Proclamation**: An official or public announcement, often made in a formal manner.
  Example: The president made a **proclamation** about the new national holiday.
- **Acclaim**: To praise enthusiastically and publicly.
  Example: The film received widespread **acclaim** for its innovative storytelling.

Word Duel: Clamor vs. Acclaim

Question: Which word refers to loud public outcry or protest?
A.) Clamor
B.) Acclaim

Correct Answer: Clamor

Explanation: **Clamor** refers to loud, insistent demands or protests, often from a group. **Acclaim**, on the other hand, refers to enthusiastic praise or approval, often in a more positive context.

Semantic Scale: Expressions of Sound

This scale shows words related to vocal expressions, from strong protests to enthusiastic approval:

1. **Whisper**: A soft, hushed voice or sound.
   Example: They shared secrets in a quiet **whisper**.
2. **Murmur**: A low, continuous sound or speech.
   Example: The crowd began to **murmur** with excitement as the event approached.
3. **Exclaim**: A sudden, loud cry or expression of strong emotion.
   Example: She **exclaimed** in joy upon hearing the good news.
4. **Clamor**: A loud outcry, often from many voices, usually in protest or demand.
   Example: There was a **clamor** for justice after the incident.
5. **Proclamation**: A formal, public announcement.
   Example: The **proclamation** of new laws was broadcasted on the radio.
6. **Acclaim**: Enthusiastic and public praise.
   Example: The actor received wide **acclaim** for his performance in the film.

Brief Story: The Power of a Shout

In the small town of Hillcrest, a **clamor** was rising. The people were frustrated with the new policies that had been enacted by the local government. One evening, as the town square filled with residents, a loud and insistent cry echoed through the streets. The people gathered in protest, demanding change.

At the front of the crowd stood Mayor Thompson, who raised his hands to get their attention. "I understand your concerns," he began, his voice firm but calm. "We will make sure your voices are heard."

He then made a **proclamation** to the crowd, assuring them that a committee would be formed to review the policies. The crowd, still vocal but hopeful, quieted down to listen. After his speech, the mayor was met with **acclaim** from those who were pleased with his actions. Others, however, continued to **exclaim** their frustrations, unwilling to settle for just words.

Despite the ongoing **clamor**, the mayor knew the importance of listening to his people and vowed to act on their concerns. Through his efforts, the community learned that change often begins with a single loud call, followed by a concerted effort to turn outcry into meaningful progress.

ROOT: "POLY-" (MEANING: "MANY")

Origin:
The root **"poly-"** comes from the Greek word **"polys,"** meaning **"many"** or **"multiple."** It is used in words that describe things involving many parts, elements, or individuals, often emphasizing diversity or multiplicity.

Vocabulary:
- **Polygon**: A shape with many sides.
  Example: The artist drew a **polygon** with eight sides for the design.
- **Polyglot**: A person who knows and is able to use several languages.
  Example: She is a fluent **polyglot**, speaking five languages fluently.
- **Polygamy**: The practice of having more than one spouse at the same time.
  Example: In some cultures, **polygamy** is still practiced, where men have multiple wives.
- **Polytheism**: The belief in or worship of multiple gods.
  Example: Ancient Greek religion was based on **polytheism**, with gods like Zeus and Hera.

Word Duel: Polyglot vs. Monolingual
Question: Which term describes someone who speaks multiple languages?

A.) Polyglot
B.) Monolingual

Correct Answer: Polyglot

Explanation: A **polyglot** is a person who speaks several languages, while **monolingual** refers to someone who speaks only one language.

Semantic Scale: Types of Beliefs

This scale shows words related to belief systems, from monotheism to polytheism:

1. **Monotheism**: The belief in a single god.
   Example: Christianity, Judaism, and Islam are all monotheistic religions.
2. **Polytheism**: The belief in multiple gods.
   Example: **Polytheism** was practiced in ancient Egypt, with gods like Ra and Anubis.
3. **Pantheism**: The belief that the universe and God are identical.
   Example: In **pantheism**, everything in nature is seen as part of the divine.
4. **Atheism**: The belief in no gods.
   Example: **Atheism** is the rejection of belief in any deity.
5. **Agnosticism**: The view that the existence of gods is unknown or unknowable.
   Example: An **agnostic** is uncertain about the existence of a higher power.

Story: The Village of Many Voices

In the village of Langlea, there was a man named Elias who was known far and wide as a **polyglot**. He could speak seven languages fluently, having learned them as a child when his family moved to different parts of the world. Elias had a gift for understanding different cultures, which made him an invaluable asset to the village.

One day, the village elders gathered to discuss a matter of great importance: the future of their land. Some wanted to adopt **polytheism**, believing that multiple gods could protect their village, while others held onto the old traditions of **monotheism**, worshiping a single, all-powerful god.

As the debate grew heated, Elias stood up and spoke in several languages, trying to unite the people with words of wisdom. "We are all united in our diversity," he said, "whether we believe in many gods or one, it is the spirit of unity that will guide us."

The village recognized that their strength lay not in the number of gods they worshipped, but in their shared values and respect for each other. While some still practiced **polygamy** in the village, others preferred monogamous marriages, but they all worked together in harmony.

The village learned that the true power of community comes from the **many** voices that speak, each contributing their unique wisdom to the greater whole.

ROOT: "SENT-" (MEANING: "FEEL" OR "THINK")

Origin:
The root **"sent-"** comes from the Latin word **"sentire,"** meaning **"to feel"** or **"to perceive."** It appears in words related to emotions, feelings, and thinking, as well as the senses.

Vocabulary:
- **Sentiment**: A feeling or emotion, often about something personal or specific.
  Example: His words were full of **sentiment**, showing how much he cared for her.
- **Consent**: To give permission or agree to something.
  Example: She gave her **consent** to the proposal after careful consideration.
- **Sensory**: Relating to the senses, such as sight, hearing, touch, taste, and smell.
  Example: The **sensory** experience of the concert was overwhelming, with vibrant lights and powerful music.
- **Dissent**: To disagree with or oppose an idea or decision.
  Example: Despite the majority's opinion, she expressed her **dissent** on the matter.

Word Duel: Sentiment vs. Dissent
Question: Which word describes an expression of feeling or emotion?
  A.) Sentiment

B.) Dissent

Correct Answer: Sentiment

Explanation: Sentiment refers to feelings or emotions, often expressed in a thoughtful way, while **dissent** refers to expressing disagreement or opposition, especially in a formal or public way.

Semantic Scale: Expressions of Agreement and Disagreement

This scale shows words related to agreement and disagreement, from silent assent to strong opposition:

1. **Consent**: To agree or give permission.
   Example: She gave her **consent** to the new rules.
2. **Assent**: To express agreement, typically in a formal way.
   Example: The committee nodded in **assent** after hearing the proposal.
3. **Dissent**: To disagree or express a differing opinion.
   Example: Several members **dissented** from the proposed policy.
4. **Protest**: A stronger expression of objection or resistance.
   Example: The workers organized a **protest** against the unfair treatment.
5. **Revolt**: A more intense form of dissent, often involving active resistance.
   Example: The people began to **revolt** against the oppressive regime.

Brief Story: The Town's Divided Opinion

In the town of Clearwater, there was a lively debate about whether to build a new park in the heart of the town. Some townspeople were enthusiastic about the project, seeing it as a place for families to gather and children to play. These individuals shared a **sentiment** of joy and excitement about the prospect of a new space to enjoy nature.

However, not everyone agreed. A group of residents

expressed their **dissent**, arguing that the park would take away much-needed parking space for local businesses. They felt the project would harm the community rather than help it.

The mayor, understanding the importance of hearing all voices, called a town meeting to discuss the matter further. After listening to both sides, she asked for **consent** from the residents to proceed with a vote on the park. As the discussion unfolded, the sensory experience of hearing both passionate support and strong opposition became evident, showing just how deeply people felt about the issue.

In the end, the community reached a compromise, incorporating the concerns of the dissenters while maintaining the excitement of the proponents. The project went forward, with everyone recognizing the value of considering both **sentiment** and **dissent** in shaping a solution.

ROOT: "FRACT-" (MEANING: "BREAK")

Origin:
The root **"fract-"** comes from the Latin word **"frangere,"** meaning **"to break"** or **"to shatter."** It appears in words related to breaking, splitting, or dividing something into parts.

Vocabulary:
- **Fraction**: A part or portion of a whole, typically expressed as a number divided by another.
  Example: One-half is a **fraction** of the whole pizza.
- **Fracture**: A break or crack, especially in bones or other solid materials.
  Example: He suffered a **fracture** in his arm after the fall.
- **Infraction**: A violation or breach of a law, rule, or agreement.
  Example: He received a penalty for his **infraction** of the traffic laws.
- **Refract**: To bend or change the direction of light or another wave as it passes through a medium.
  Example: The light was **refracted** as it passed through the prism, creating a rainbow.

Word Duel: Fraction vs. Fracture
Question: Which word refers to a break or crack in something?
  A.) Fraction

B.) Fracture
Correct Answer: Fracture
Explanation: A **fracture** refers to a break, often used in the context of bones or solid materials, while a **fraction** is a part of a whole, typically in mathematical terms.

Semantic Scale: Types of Breaks
This scale shows different types of breaks, from minor to severe:
- **Fraction**: A small part or portion of a whole.
  Example: A **fraction** of the pie was left after the party.
- **Infraction**: A minor violation or breach, typically of a rule or law.
  Example: A speeding ticket is an **infraction**.
- **Fracture**: A more serious break, often in a bone or object.
  Example: The **fracture** in the glass was caused by the impact.
- **Break**: A more general term for something splitting or being divided.
  Example: He took a short **break** from his work to get some fresh air.
- **Rupture**: A severe or violent break, often sudden and destructive.
  Example: The **rupture** of the pipe caused a flood in the basement.

Brief Story: The Broken Bridge
　　In the small village of Hillview, a bridge connected the two parts of the town across the river. One day, a heavy truck crossed the bridge, and a **fracture** appeared in one of the support beams. The bridge was now unsafe, and the town needed to act quickly.
　　The mayor called a meeting to discuss the repairs. Some residents wanted to **fraction** the cost and only repair the most essential parts, while others argued that the whole bridge needed to be fixed to prevent further damage. As the debate continued, a traffic **infraction** occurred when a driver ignored

the closed bridge signs and tried to cross.

A group of engineers arrived to inspect the damage. They explained that they would need to **refract** the light in the testing equipment to assess the depth of the **fracture**. After thorough analysis, they decided the bridge would need to be fully rebuilt to prevent a potential **rupture** during the next storm.

The community came together to raise the necessary funds, agreeing that safety was more important than saving a fraction of the cost. The bridge was repaired, and the villagers learned the importance of acting before a **fracture** became a **rupture**, and how working together could fix what had been broken.

ROOT: "GEN-" (MEANING: "BIRTH" OR "RACE")

Origin:
The root **"gen-"** comes from the Latin word **"genera,"** meaning **"birth," "race,"** or **"kind."** It appears in words related to origins, creation, and the transmission of traits or characteristics, especially in biology, family, and culture.

Vocabulary:
- **Generate**: To produce or create something.
  Example: The company aims to **generate** new ideas for sustainable energy solutions.
- **Generation**: A group of individuals born and living around the same time, or the act of producing offspring.
  Example: The **generation** that lived through World War II has a unique perspective on history.
- **Genealogy**: The study of family history and the tracing of ancestors.
  Example: She researched her **genealogy** and discovered that her great-grandfather immigrated from Ireland.
- **Genetic**: Relating to genes or heredity, often passed down from parents to offspring.
  Example: **Genetic** factors play a significant role in determining a person's eye color.

Word Duel: Generate vs. Genealogy
Question: Which word is used to describe the study of family

history?
   A.) Generate
   B.) Genealogy

Correct Answer: Genealogy

Explanation: Genealogy refers to the study or tracing of family ancestry, while **generate** means to create or produce something, often used in contexts like energy production or idea creation.

Sources of Origin

This list shows words related to origins or the beginning of something, from biological birth to creation:

1. **Generate**: To produce or create something from a source.
   Example: The factory can **generate** thousands of products a day.
2. **Procreate**: To create offspring or children.
   Example: Many animals **procreate** during the spring season.
3. **Genealogy**: The study of family heritage and ancestry.
   Example: The **genealogy** research revealed that she was descended from a long line of scholars.
4. **Generation**: The group of people born around the same time, or the act of producing offspring.
   Example: The younger **generation** is more tech-savvy than the older one.
5. **Genetic**: Related to genes, heredity, or inherited traits.
   Example: **Genetic** disorders can sometimes be passed down through families.

Story: The Family Tree

   In the town of Greenfield, the Thompson family had lived for generations. One day, young Emma decided to learn more about her ancestors and began to study her **genealogy**. She was surprised to discover that her great-great-grandfather had been a pioneer who helped build the town's first school.

Emma's mother often spoke about **generations** of Thompsons who had been teachers, so Emma felt inspired to **generate** her own path in education. She enrolled in a local college to study teaching and dreamed of one day passing on the knowledge she received to future **generations**.

While exploring her family's roots, Emma learned about the **genetic** traits that ran through her family. It turned out that her grandmother had a talent for painting, which Emma inherited as well. Emma realized that her family history was not only shaped by the stories of those who came before her but also by the **genetic** legacy passed down through the years.

As Emma traced her family history, she marveled at how the **generation** before her had made the same choices, shaping her own journey. With her studies and the knowledge of her **genealogy**, Emma felt ready to **generate** her future, carrying on the legacy of her ancestors with pride.

ROOT: "PAN-" (MEANING: "ALL" OR "EVERY")

Origin:
The root **"pan-"** comes from the Greek word **"pan,"** meaning **"all"** or **"every."** It appears in words that convey the idea of encompassing everything or a wide range, often used in contexts where something covers a large scope, is universal, or affects everything.

Vocabulary:
- **Panorama**: A wide, all-encompassing view of an area or scene.
  Example: The mountaintop offered a breathtaking **panorama** of the entire valley below.
- **Pandemic**: A widespread disease that affects large portions of the population, often worldwide.
  Example: The COVID-19 **pandemic** changed the way people live and interact globally.
- **Panacea**: A universal remedy or solution for all problems or difficulties.
  Example: Some people believe that technology can be a **panacea** for all social issues, but it isn't always the answer.
- **Pantheon**: A collection of gods, or more broadly, a group of highly respected individuals in a particular field.
  Example: Shakespeare is considered part of the literary **pantheon** because of his lasting influence on English

literature.

Word Duel: Panacea vs. Pandemic

Question: Which word refers to a widespread disease?

    A.) Panacea

    B.) Pandemic

Correct Answer: Pandemic

Explanation: A **pandemic** refers to a disease that spreads widely across multiple countries or continents, while **panacea** refers to a solution or remedy that is believed to solve all problems, not a disease.

Semantic Scale: Range of Coverage

This scale shows words related to the scope or range of something, from limited to all-encompassing:

1. **Partial**: A small or limited part of something.
   Example: The **partial** view from the window only showed the nearby street.
2. **Comprehensive**: Including all or nearly all elements.
   Example: The report gave a **comprehensive** analysis of the current economic situation.
3. **Panorama**: A complete, unbroken view or representation of something in its entirety.
   Example: The photographer captured a stunning **panorama** of the coastline at sunset.
4. **Universal**: Affecting or relating to everyone or everything.
   Example: The desire for happiness is a **universal** human experience.
5. **Panacea**: A supposed universal cure or solution for all problems.
   Example: While exercise is beneficial, it is not a **panacea** for every health issue.

Story: The Wide Horizon

    Emma had always loved hiking and often sought out the most beautiful and expansive views. On her latest trip to the mountains, she reached a high point that offered a perfect

panorama of the entire valley. From the peak, she could see everything—vast fields, small towns, and winding rivers. The sight took her breath away as it felt as though she could see the world in its entirety.

However, her journey was not without challenges. Along the way, Emma had heard rumors of a **pandemic** sweeping across the country, affecting millions. It was a reminder that while the world might seem vast and beautiful, it was also connected and vulnerable. Emma hoped that a **panacea** for such global problems would soon be found, but she knew it would take more than one solution to heal such widespread issues.

On her hike, Emma met other travelers from different parts of the world. She was struck by how people from all backgrounds and cultures could come together in nature, and for a moment, she felt part of a greater **pantheon** of people who shared the same desire to explore, learn, and understand the world around them. Each of them contributed to the ever-expanding story of human experience, just like every part of the **panorama** before her.

ROOT: "PATER-" (MEANING: "FATHER")

Origin:
The root **"pater-"** comes from the Latin word **"pater,"** meaning **"father."** It appears in words that are associated with fatherhood, authority, or influence. The root often carries a sense of leadership or responsibility, particularly in relation to family or community roles.

Vocabulary:
- **Paternity**: The state of being a father, or the relationship between a father and his child.
  Example: The DNA test confirmed his **paternity** of the child.
- **Patriarch**: The male head of a family, tribe, or group, often considered a respected leader.
  Example: The **patriarch** of the family was known for his wisdom and generosity.
- **Patron**: A person who supports or sponsors an individual, organization, or cause, often with financial help.
  Example: The museum's new exhibition was funded by a generous **patron**.
- **Expatriate**: A person who lives outside their native country, often for work or personal reasons. The term comes from the idea of being removed from one's "fatherland."

Example: After years of living abroad, Mark became an **expatriate** in France, never quite feeling like he belonged in his homeland anymore.

Word Duel: Patron vs. Expatriate

Question: Which word refers to someone who supports an organization or cause, often with financial help?

  A.) Patron
  B.) Expatriate

Correct Answer: Patron

Explanation: A **patron** is a supporter or sponsor of a cause, organization, or person, especially through financial support. An **expatriate**, on the other hand, refers to someone who lives outside their native country.

Authority and Influence

This scale shows words related to authority or leadership, from family roles to broader societal influence:

1. **Patriarch**: A senior male figure in a family, often a revered leader. Note that Matriarch can be used for a female in a similar position.
   Example: The **patriarch** of the company was instrumental in its growth.
2. **Patron**: A person who provides financial or moral support, often in cultural or artistic contexts.
   Example: The artist thanked her **patrons** for making her exhibition possible.
3. **Expatriate**: A person living outside their homeland, often distanced from familial or national authority.
   Example: The **expatriate** community in the city offered each other support as they adapted to new lives abroad.

Story: A Family's Legacy

In the small town of Meadowbrook, the **patriarch** of the Miller family, Grandpa George, was a well-respected figure. His wisdom and decisions shaped the lives of his children and grandchildren, and his guidance was sought by many in the community. He was a symbol of leadership, much like the **father** of a household who ensures that each member thrives.

When George passed, his eldest son, Henry, took on the role of **patriarch**, continuing his father's legacy by leading the family business and keeping the traditions alive. His **paternity** was never questioned, and he embraced his role with pride and responsibility.

A wealthy **patron** who had once been helped by George returned to offer a large donation to the local school. The **patron** had remembered the kindness George had shown him years ago, and in turn, he wanted to give back to the community.

Meanwhile, George's grandson, Tom, decided to move abroad for work and became an **expatriate**. Although he missed his family deeply, he felt his journey was necessary for his career and personal growth. Still, he remained in touch with his roots, honoring the **paternal** legacy left by his grandfather and father.

ROOT: "PEL-" (MEANING: "DRIVE" OR "PUSH")

Origin:
The root **"pel-"** comes from the Latin verb **"pellere,"** meaning **"to drive"** or **"to push."** It appears in words that convey the idea of pushing, driving, or forcing movement, either physically or metaphorically. The root emphasizes action and motion, often relating to the exertion of force or influence.

Vocabulary:
- **Propel**: To push or drive something forward, often with force.
  Example: The powerful engine **propelled** the boat across the water at high speed.
- **Compel**: To force someone to do something, often through pressure or persuasion.
  Example: His sense of duty **compelled** him to volunteer for the challenging task.
- **Expel**: To drive out or force someone to leave, often from a group or organization.
  Example: The school decided to **expel** the student after repeated violations of the rules.
- **Repel**: To drive something or someone away, often with force or resistance.
  Example: The strong winds **repelled** the approaching storm clouds, delaying the rain.

Word Duel: Compel vs. Repel
Question: Which word means to force someone to do something against their will?
    A.) Compel
    B.) Repel
Correct Answer: **Compel**
Explanation: **Compel** means to force someone to act or behave in a certain way, often against their own desires or free will. **Repel**, on the other hand, means to push something away or resist it, often in a physical sense.

Semantic Scale: Influence and Force
This scale shows words related to different levels of pushing, driving, or forcing, from mild influence to strong action:

1. **Encourage**: To inspire or motivate someone to take action.
   Example: His teacher **encouraged** him to pursue his artistic talents.
2. **Persuade**: To convince someone to do something through reasoning or argument.
   Example: She tried to **persuade** him to join the team by highlighting the benefits.
3. **Compel**: To force someone to act, often due to strong pressure or external factors.
   Example: The urgency of the situation **compelled** him to make a decision quickly.
4. **Propel**: To drive something forward with force, often implying motion or speed.
   Example: The rocket engines **propelled** the spacecraft into orbit.
5. **Expel**: To force someone to leave or be removed from a place or group.
   Example: The coach decided to **expel** the player for breaking team rules.
6. **Repel**: To drive or force something away, often implying resistance or defense.

Example: The guard dogs were trained to **repel** any intruders.

Story: The Push for Change

Samantha had always been a quiet person, but one particular event **compelled** her to take action. After seeing the environmental destruction caused by the recent wildfire, she knew she had to make a change. The sense of urgency **propelled** her to start a local campaign to raise awareness about climate change. She began organizing meetings, gathering support, and speaking to anyone who would listen.

However, not everyone agreed with her views. Some skeptics tried to **repel** her efforts by spreading misinformation, but Samantha refused to back down. She believed that even if it was difficult, she had a responsibility to push for positive change.

Soon, her message began to gain traction. People who were once indifferent now saw the importance of the issue, and the community rallied behind her cause. The local authorities, realizing the strength of the movement, began to take action as well, forcing the opposition to **expel** their negative campaign. Samantha had learned the power of perseverance, and her ability to **propel** a community into action was the driving force behind the change that followed.

ROOT: "SOCI-" (MEANING: "COMPANION" OR "SOCIETY")

Origin:
The root **"soci-"** comes from the Latin word **"socius,"** meaning **"companion"** or **"ally."** It appears in words that are related to social interactions, companionship, or community. The root emphasizes the idea of connection, association, and the relationships between individuals within a group or society.

Vocabulary:
- **Social**: Relating to society or the interactions between individuals within a group.
  Example: The community held a **social** event to celebrate the harvest festival.
- **Sociable**: Friendly and inclined to engage in conversation or social interaction.
  Example: Tom is a very **sociable** person; he enjoys meeting new people and making friends.
- **Sociology**: The study of society, social behavior, and human interactions within groups.
  Example: She decided to major in **sociology** to understand how different cultures shape social behavior.
- **Antisocial**: Avoiding or not enjoying social interaction with others; often unfriendly or withdrawn.

Example: His **antisocial** behavior at the party made everyone uncomfortable, as he preferred to stay by himself.

Word Duel: Sociable vs. Antisocial

Question: Which word describes a person who enjoys and seeks social interactions with others?

    A.) Sociable
    B.) Antisocial

Correct Answer: Sociable

Explanation: A **sociable** person is friendly and enjoys interacting with others. An **antisocial** person, on the other hand, tends to avoid social situations and prefers solitude or minimal interaction with others.

Semantic Scale: Social Interaction

This scale shows words related to the range of social engagement, from active participation to withdrawal:

1. **Sociable**: Enjoys engaging with others, often friendly and outgoing.
   Example: She's always **sociable** at gatherings and makes an effort to talk to everyone.
2. **Social**: Pertaining to society or group interactions, often indicating participation in communal activities.
   Example: The **social** aspect of the event made it lively and fun for all attendees.
3. **Antisocial**: Avoiding or shunning social interactions, often displaying reluctance to engage.
   Example: His **antisocial** tendencies were evident when he refused to attend the reunion.

Brief Story: A Sociable Gathering

    At the annual neighborhood picnic, Emma was the life of the party. Her **sociable** nature made her the center of attention as she moved from group to group, chatting with everyone. Whether it was sharing jokes, exchanging stories, or simply listening to others, she made everyone feel comfortable and welcomed.

On the other side of the park, Mark, a more **antisocial** individual, sat quietly under a tree. He didn't mind the company of others but preferred not to participate in the lively conversations. Despite his **antisocial** demeanor, he found solace in observing the bustling social dynamics around him.

As the day went on, a few people tried to engage Mark, but he politely declined. Emma, ever the **sociable** host, noticed his solitude and decided to join him for a quiet conversation, bridging the gap between their differing social styles.

Though they had contrasting approaches to socializing, they both appreciated the value of community. Emma loved to engage with others, while Mark enjoyed the peacefulness of observing from a distance, but together they understood that **socius**—companionship—was at the heart of any social gathering.

ROOT: "PEND-" (MEANING: "HANG" OR "WEIGH")

Origin:
The root **"pend-"** comes from the Latin verb **"pendere,"** meaning **"to hang"** or **"to weigh."** It appears in words that refer to hanging, suspension, or weighing in a figurative or literal sense. This root emphasizes the idea of something being suspended in place or balanced, either physically or in terms of importance or consideration.

Vocabulary:
- **Suspend**: To hang something from above or temporarily stop something from continuing.
  Example: The school decided to **suspend** the classes for the day due to the snowstorm.
- **Depend**: To rely on something or someone for support or outcome.
  Example: Her success in the competition **depends** on how well she performs in the final round.
- **Pendant**: A piece of jewelry that hangs from a chain, often worn around the neck.
  Example: She wore a beautiful silver **pendant** that had been passed down through generations.
- **Expend**: To spend or use up something, often referring to resources such as time, energy, or money.
  Example: They had to **expend** all their energy in

preparing for the long hike ahead.

Word Duel: Depend vs. Expend

Question: Which word means to use or consume something, such as time or resources?

    A.) Depend
    B.) Expend

Correct Answer: Expend

Explanation: **Expend** refers to spending or using up something, particularly in terms of energy or resources. **Depend**, on the other hand, means to rely on something or someone for support or outcome.

Semantic Scale: Levels of Suspension and Reliance

This scale shows words related to the concept of suspension, reliance, and expenditure:

1. **Pend** (Base form): To hang or suspend.
   Example: The decorations **pend** gracefully from the ceiling.
2. **Suspend**: To temporarily stop or hang something in a state of pause or interruption.
   Example: The match was **suspended** due to heavy rain.
3. **Depend**: To rely or be contingent upon something.
   Example: Your grade in the class will **depend** on your final project submission.
4. **Expend**: To use up, often in terms of resources such as energy or money.
   Example: They **expend** considerable effort to maintain their garden year-round.

Story: The Weight of Choices

    Emma found herself at a crossroads. The decision to move to another city for her job opportunity seemed exciting, but it also left her feeling uncertain. She had to **depend** on the advice of her friends and family, knowing that their perspectives would influence her choice. Yet, the weight of the decision felt heavy, as if she were **suspended** in the air, unable to move one way or the other.

Her mentor, seeing her indecision, gave her a **pendant** as a reminder: "Every decision has weight, but you must trust yourself to make it." Emma took this to heart, but she knew that to achieve her goals, she would need to **expend** the effort to embrace new challenges.

After much reflection, she chose to move forward with the job. She felt lighter, no longer **suspended** between options. Emma had relied on her inner strength and the support of those around her to make the right decision.

ROOT: "LOG-" (MEANING: "WORD" OR "STUDY")

Origin:
The root **"log-"** comes from the Greek word **"logos,"** which means **"word," "speech,"** or **"reason."** It is often found in words related to reasoning, speech, or the study of a particular subject. Over time, this root evolved to represent the concept of speech or discourse and the scientific or intellectual study of specific topics.

Vocabulary:
- **Logic**: The study of reasoning, principles of valid inference, and the correct use of reasoning in argumentation.
  Example: The philosopher studied **logic** to better understand the structure of rational thought.
- **Dialogue**: A conversation between two or more people, or the exchange of ideas or opinions.
  Example: The **dialogue** between the two characters in the play highlighted the conflict between tradition and change.
- **Monologue**: A long speech by one person, often used in theater or literature to express a character's thoughts or emotions.
  Example: The actor delivered a powerful **monologue** that captivated the audience.

- **Biology**: The scientific study of living organisms and life processes.
  Example: She majored in **biology** because of her fascination with the diversity of life on Earth.

Word Duel: Dialogue vs. Monologue
Question: Which word refers to a conversation between two or more people?
   A.) Dialogue
   B.) Monologue
Correct Answer: Dialogue
Explanation: A **dialogue** involves an exchange of ideas between two or more people, while a **monologue** is a long speech given by one person, often without interaction from others.

Levels of Communication
This list shows words related to communication, from individual speech to collaborative exchange:
1. **Monologue**: A speech delivered by one person, often expressing deep thoughts or emotions.
   Example: The actor's **monologue** revealed the inner turmoil of the character.
2. **Dialogue**: A conversation between two or more individuals, often creating interaction and exchange.
   Example: The **dialogue** between the students helped them reach a consensus on the project.
3. **Logic**: The study or use of reasoning to support arguments or conclusions.
   Example: The debate was structured around sound **logic** and careful analysis of facts.

Story: The Power of Words
At the university's annual symposium, Dr. Roberts gave a **monologue** on the importance of understanding **logic** in our daily lives. He spoke passionately about how reasoning shapes our decisions, and how logical thought can be applied to

everything from personal choices to global issues. His speech was compelling, but the real impact came later during the **dialogue** session, where attendees could ask questions and discuss his points.

In the **dialogue** that followed, students engaged with the professor, offering their own perspectives and challenging his conclusions. One student, Maria, used **logic** to refute a point Dr. Roberts made about environmental policies. Her argument, based on well-reasoned principles, left the professor thinking deeply.

The exchange of ideas through **dialogue** and **monologue** at the symposium demonstrated the power of words to not only inform but to inspire thoughtful reflection and debate. In the end, everyone walked away with new insights, understanding that **logos**—the study of reasoning and the use of words—was not just academic but vital in shaping the world.

ROOT: "ACT-" (MEANING: "DO" OR "DRIVE")

Origin:
The root **"act-"** comes from the Latin verb **"agere,"** meaning **"to do," "to drive,"** or **"to perform."** This root appears in words related to doing something, whether it is performing an action, reacting to something, or taking steps to create change. Over time, this root evolved to reflect movement, influence, and the act of bringing something into existence or motion.

Vocabulary:
- **Action**: The process of doing something, typically to achieve a result.
  Example: The committee decided to take **action** after hearing the urgent report.
- **React**: To respond or behave in response to something that happens.
  Example: The team had to **react** quickly when the power went out during the presentation.
- **Enact**: To make something happen, usually through official means, such as passing laws.
  Example: The government decided to **enact** new policies to address the growing environmental crisis.
- **Actor**: A person who performs in plays, movies, or television shows, embodying characters through their actions.

Example: The **actor** won several awards for his compelling portrayal of a historical figure.

Word Duel: Action vs. React

Question: Which word refers to responding to a stimulus or situation?

    A.) Action

    B.) React

Correct Answer: React

Explanation: **React** refers to responding to an external stimulus or situation, often with immediate or reflexive action. **Action**, on the other hand, refers to a deliberate or intentional act or movement.

Semantic Scale: Levels of Activity

This scale shows words related to action, from performing something deliberate to responding reflexively:

1. **Actor**: A person who performs and embodies a role, often bringing something to life through actions.
   Example: The **actor** portrayed a complex character in the drama series.
2. **Action**: The process of performing an act or doing something, often aimed at achieving a specific goal.
   Example: Her **action** in organizing the event made a positive impact on the community.
3. **Enact**: To make something official, such as a law, by taking action in a formal context.
   Example: The board voted to **enact** new regulations to improve workplace safety.
4. **React**: To respond or behave in reaction to an event or situation.
   Example: He had to **react** quickly to the sudden change in plans.

Brief Story: The Power of Action

    In a small town, the citizens had been hearing reports about a nearby river's pollution. At first, everyone was hesitant to **act**, unsure of how to handle the problem. However, when a group of concerned individuals decided to take **action**, they organized a cleanup initiative and began spreading awareness about the importance of preserving the river.

The town's mayor, seeing the impact of the initiative, decided to **enact** a new policy that would help regulate waste management in the area. But as the day of the cleanup event approached, a storm unexpectedly hit. The volunteers had to **react** quickly, moving supplies to a sheltered area to keep the event going despite the rain.

One of the volunteers, an **actor** by profession, took it upon himself to rally the community, giving a speech that inspired others to join the cause. Thanks to their **actions**, the town's river was cleaned, and the new policy was successfully enacted, showing the importance of taking initiative and responding to challenges.

ROOT: "MAN-" (MEANING: "HAND")

Origin:
The root **"man-"** comes from the Latin word **"manus,"** which means **"hand."** This root is found in words related to the use or control of the hands, whether it's doing something by hand, creating something, or controlling or influencing through actions. Over time, it expanded to represent manual work, craftsmanship, and the manipulation of objects or situations.

Vocabulary:
- **Manual**: Done with the hands or requiring physical effort.
  Example: The workers followed a **manual** to assemble the furniture step by step.
- **Manufacture**: To make or create something, especially in large quantities, often with machinery.
  Example: The company began to **manufacture** electronic devices for the global market.
- **Manipulate**: To control or handle something, often with skill, and sometimes with a connotation of control or influence over others.
  Example: He tried to **manipulate** the situation to his advantage, but his plans were exposed.
- **Manicure**: A cosmetic treatment for the hands and nails, usually involving cutting, shaping, and polishing.
  Example: She treated herself to a **manicure** before her big

interview.

Word Duel: Manual vs. Manufacture
Question: Which word refers to the process of making something by hand, especially in large quantities?
   A.) Manual
   B.) Manufacture
Correct Answer: Manufacture
Explanation: **Manufacture** refers to the process of making goods, typically in large quantities and often using machines. **Manual** refers to something done by hand or requiring physical labor, but it does not necessarily imply mass production.

Hand-Related Work
This list shows words related to manual effort, from personal handwork to industrial production:
1. **Manicure**: A personal, often delicate treatment involving the hands and nails.
   Example: She booked a **manicure** for a relaxing afternoon.
2. **Manual**: Physical work done by hand, usually indicating effort and craftsmanship.
   Example: The car mechanic explained that the **manual** repairs were more time-consuming.
3. **Manipulate**: To control or manage something skillfully, often with hands, but also in a figurative sense.
   Example: The artist learned to **manipulate** the clay to create intricate sculptures.
4. **Manufacture**: The process of making or producing something, especially on a large scale using machinery.
   Example: The company invested in new technology to **manufacture** parts faster and more efficiently.

Brief Story: The Power of the Hand
   Sarah had always loved **manual** work, finding

satisfaction in using her hands to create beautiful pieces of art. As a child, she would spend hours sculpting clay figures, a skill she later refined into pottery. When she grew older, she decided to **manufacture** her own pottery line, hoping to bring her craftsmanship to a wider audience.

However, the challenges of running a business soon emerged. To succeed, she had to **manipulate** the market, using her connections and advertising skills to make her products more appealing. She also ensured that her products were of the highest quality by using only the best materials, giving each piece the same care she had taken in her childhood hobby.

One day, after finishing a large batch of pottery, Sarah decided to treat herself to a **manicure**, appreciating the simple joys that allowed her to recharge and continue creating with her hands. Her hands had built her business, and now she understood how important it was to nurture them with a bit of self-care.

Root: "nov-" (Meaning: "New")

Origin:
The root **"nov-"** comes from the Latin word **"novus,"** meaning **"new."** This root is often found in words associated with newness, whether it refers to something recently created, a person who is new to a particular skill or area, or the process of making something new. Over time, this root expanded to include concepts related to change, fresh starts, and innovation.

Vocabulary:
- **Novel**: A long work of fiction that is new or original in its form or content.
  Example: She wrote a **novel** that became a bestseller, capturing the hearts of readers with its unique storyline.
- **Novice**: A person who is new to a particular field or

activity and lacks experience.
Example: As a **novice** at painting, he eagerly sought advice from more experienced artists.

- **Renovate**: To restore or improve something, especially a building, by making it new again.
Example: They decided to **renovate** the old house to make it more modern and comfortable.
- **Innovation**: The introduction of something new, often referring to new ideas, methods, or devices.
Example: The company prides itself on its constant **innovation** in the tech industry, always striving to develop the next big breakthrough.

Word Duel: Novel vs. Novice

Question: Which word refers to a person who is new to a particular activity or field?

A.) Novel
B.) Novice

Correct Answer: Novice

Explanation: **Novice** refers to someone who is new to an activity or skill and lacks experience. On the other hand, **novel** typically refers to something new or original, especially in the context of fiction.

Semantic Scale: Levels of Newness

This scale shows words related to newness, from a fresh creation to a beginner experience:

1. **Novel**: Something new or unique, often in the context of a creative work, like a book or idea.
   Example: The **novel** approach to problem-solving changed the company's workflow.
2. **Novice**: A beginner or someone who is new to a particular skill or activity.
   Example: As a **novice** cook, she was still learning how to follow complex recipes.
3. **Renovate**: To make something old like new again, often referring to buildings or structures.

Example: They hired a contractor to **renovate** the kitchen and give it a more modern look.
4. **Innovation**: A breakthrough or new development that introduces something improved or radically different.
Example: The **innovation** of electric cars has revolutionized the automobile industry.

Story: The Fresh Start

John had always loved working with his hands, but he was a **novice** when it came to woodworking. His grandfather, a skilled carpenter, had passed down a small, worn-out workshop to him. John decided to **renovate** it, hoping to breathe new life into the place where his grandfather had spent so many years crafting furniture.

As John worked, he found that his **innovation** didn't just apply to the workshop—it applied to his craft as well. He began experimenting with new techniques and tools, striving to create **novel** designs that hadn't been seen before.

In just a few months, John's efforts were rewarded. The newly renovated workshop became a center of creativity, and his **novel** creations attracted attention. His reputation grew as he went from a **novice** to a respected craftsman, constantly evolving and pushing the boundaries of traditional woodworking.

ROOT: "SECT-" (MEANING: "CUT" OR "SEPARATE")

Origin:
The root **"sect-"** comes from the Latin word **"secare,"** meaning **"to cut"** or **"to separate."** This root is used in words that involve dividing, cutting, or separating something into parts. It often appears in contexts where things are being divided or analyzed in detail, such as in geometry, biology, or discussions about dividing groups or ideas.

Vocabulary:
- **Section**: A distinct part or division of something, often cut or separated from the whole.
  Example: The **section** of the book on history was particularly interesting.
- **Dissect**: To cut apart or analyze in detail, especially for examination.
  Example: In biology class, we were asked to **dissect** a frog to study its internal organs.
- **Intersection**: The point at which two things, such as roads or paths, cross or meet.
  Example: The **intersection** of Main Street and Elm Avenue was very busy during rush hour.
- **Bisect**: To divide into two equal parts.

Example: The line **bisected** the rectangle into two identical halves.

Word Duel: Section vs. Dissect

Question: Which word refers to dividing something into smaller parts for analysis or examination?

A.) Section
B.) Dissect

Correct Answer: Dissect

Explanation: Dissect refers to carefully cutting apart something, often for scientific or educational analysis, such as in biology. **Section** simply refers to a part or division of a whole and doesn't imply the detailed cutting or examination that **dissect** does.

Levels of Separation

This list shows words related to cutting or dividing, from simply dividing something into parts to analyzing it in detail:

1. **Section**: A distinct part or segment of a whole.
   Example: The **section** of the park near the river is perfect for picnics.
2. **Bisect**: To divide into two equal parts, often with precision.
   Example: He **bisected** the cake to make sure each piece was the same size.
3. **Intersection**: The place where two or more things meet or cross.
   Example: The **intersection** of the two highways created a busy area for drivers.
4. **Dissect**: To cut apart and analyze something in great detail.
   Example: The students had to **dissect** the poem to fully understand its themes and meanings.

Story: The Divided Path

Emma loved studying the structure of plants, so she enrolled in a biology class where the first lesson was to **dissect** a leaf. At first, she was hesitant, but as she carefully made the cut, she marveled at how each **section** of the leaf contributed to its function.

Later in the semester, Emma learned about **intersections** in nature—the points where different species or ecosystems meet. She was fascinated by the idea of how different elements of nature **bisect** each other, creating new ecosystems where they overlap. Her newfound understanding of how life divides and merges sparked a deeper passion for environmental science.

ROOT: "REG-" (MEANING: "RULE" OR "DIRECT")

Origin:
The root **"reg-"** comes from the Latin word **"regere,"** meaning **"to rule"** or **"to direct."** It is often associated with concepts of leadership, control, governance, or order. This root appears in words related to rules, regulation, and authoritative direction.

Vocabulary:
- **Regular**: Conforming to a standard or rule; usual or habitual.
  Example: She maintains a **regular** exercise routine, working out every morning without fail.
- **Regulate**: To control or direct according to a set of rules or guidelines.
  Example: The government plans to **regulate** the use of plastic bags to reduce environmental waste.
- **Regent**: A person appointed to rule or govern in the absence of the monarch or a ruler.
  Example: During the king's absence, the **regent** ruled the kingdom with wisdom and justice.
- **Regal**: Relating to royalty or kingship; royal in nature or quality.
  Example: The ballroom was decorated with **regal** elegance, fit for a royal celebration.

Word Duel: Regular vs. Regulate

Question: Which word refers to controlling or managing something according to rules or standards?
   A.) Regular
   B.) Regulate

Correct Answer: Regulate

Explanation: **Regulate** means to control or manage something according to a set of rules or principles, while **regular** simply refers to something that occurs in a usual, habitual, or standard manner.

Semantic Scale: Levels of Control

This scale shows words related to control or leadership, from being orderly and consistent to having authority:

1. **Regular**: Consistent, habitual, or occurring at set intervals.
   Example: His **regular** meetings with clients helped to establish a solid working relationship.
2. **Regal**: Of or relating to royalty, often used to describe something grand or majestic.
   Example: The queen's **regal** presence made everyone feel in awe.
3. **Regulate**: To control or direct something according to rules or standards.
   Example: The company must **regulate** employee hours to comply with labor laws.
4. **Regent**: A ruler or leader who governs in place of someone else.
   Example: The **regent** ensured that the kingdom flourished during the king's long absence.

Brief Story: A Kingdom in Order

   In the kingdom of Arland, the king had been absent for many years, leaving the **regent** in charge. The **regent**, a wise and fair ruler, worked to **regulate** the kingdom's laws and policies, ensuring that peace and order were maintained. Under her rule, things became more **regular**; citizens knew what to expect, and life ran smoothly.

One day, the regent threw a grand feast, decorated with **regal** touches—golden chandeliers, velvet curtains, and dishes fit for royalty. The guests marveled at the beauty and order of the event, reflecting the **regal** nature of the kingdom's governance under her watch. The **regent** had done more than just maintain peace; she had made the kingdom thrive by following the rules, showing how well-ordering and leadership could bring prosperity.

ROOT: "FUG-" (MEANING: "FLEE" OR "RUN")

Origin:
The root "fug-" is derived from the Latin word "fugere," meaning "to flee" or "to run away." It appears in words related to escape, evasion, or movement from one place to another.

Vocabulary:
1. **Fugitive**: A person who is running away, especially from the law or justice.
    - Example: The fugitive escaped into the woods and was later caught by the police.
2. **Refuge**: A place or state of safety, shelter, or protection from danger or trouble.
    - Example: The refugees sought refuge in a neighboring country after the war.
3. **Fugue**: A musical composition where a theme or melody is repeated in different voices or keys. In psychology, it refers to a state of amnesia where a person forgets their identity and may travel without awareness.
    - Example: The composer's fugue was filled with intricate harmonies and shifts in tone.
4. **Subterfuge**: Deceptive strategies or actions used to achieve a goal, typically to avoid detection or gain an advantage.

- Example: The spy relied on subterfuge to infiltrate the enemy's ranks without being noticed.

Word Duel: Fugitive vs. Refuge

Question: Which word describes someone fleeing from danger or the law?

    A.) Fugitive
    B.) Refuge

Correct Answer: Fugitive

Explanation: A **fugitive** is someone who flees, typically from the law, while **refuge** is a safe place or shelter, often sought by those in danger or in need of protection.

Escaping or Seeking Safety

This list shows words ranging from fleeing to finding safety:

- **Flee** – To run away from danger or threat.
  - Example: He had to flee the scene of the accident.
- **Escape** – To break free from a place of confinement or danger.
  - Example: She managed to escape the burning building.
- **Fugitive** – Someone who is running from the law or danger.
  - Example: The fugitive was on the run for weeks before being captured.
- **Refuge** – A safe place offering shelter or protection.
  - Example: The refugees found refuge in the church during the storm.

Language Time Travel: Fugitive and Refuge

In ancient times, when people were in danger, they often sought **refuge** in fortified places, like castles or caves. The word "fugitive," on the other hand, comes from the Latin "fugere," meaning to flee, referring to someone who runs away from something, often danger or pursuit. Over time, both words have expanded to various meanings, from someone escaping justice to finding a safe haven.

The Escape

Late at night, the **fugitive** raced through the dark alleyways, his breath heavy as he dodged shadows and tried to outrun his pursuers. He had narrowly escaped from a dangerous situation, and now he was running for his life, hoping to find safety. His mind was clouded with fear, but one thought kept him going: he needed **refuge**.

As he neared the edge of the city, he spotted an abandoned building in the distance. It seemed like the perfect place to hide. When he entered, he was greeted by the eerie silence, but it was the **subterfuge** of the place—hidden rooms and secret exits—that made him feel safer.

In the corner, an old piano sat undisturbed, and as he walked past it, the soft sound of a **fugue** playing in his mind calmed him for a moment. But he knew his peace wouldn't last long. He couldn't stay here forever, and once again, he would have to flee.

ROOT: "VOL-" (MEANING: "WISH" OR "WILL")

The root "vol-" comes from the Latin word "velle," which means "to wish" or "to want." It appears in words that convey a sense of choice, desire, or willful action.

Vocabulary:
1. **Voluntary**: Done by choice or free will, not forced.
    - Example: He made a voluntary decision to help the community during the crisis.
2. **Volition**: The act of using one's will to make a decision or choice.
    - Example: She decided of her own volition to resign from the committee.
3. **Benevolent**: Having a desire to do good or act kindly.
    - Example: The benevolent organization donated large sums of money to local shelters.
4. **Volunteer**: A person who offers to do something without being paid, typically out of a desire to help.
    - Example: Many volunteers showed up to clean the park on the weekend.

Word Duel: Voluntary vs. Involuntary
Question: Which word refers to something done by choice, not by force?
   A.) Voluntary

B.) Involuntary

Correct Answer: Voluntary

Explanation: **Voluntary** comes from the root "vol-" meaning "will" or "wish," and refers to actions done by choice or free will, while **involuntary** refers to actions done without choice, typically due to reflex or compulsion.

Semantic Scale: From Willing to Forced

This scale shows words related to choice and will:

1. **Voluntary** – Done willingly or by choice.
    - Example: Her voluntary decision to donate was appreciated by the charity.
2. **Benevolent** – Acting with kindness and a desire to help others.
    - Example: The benevolent donor gave a generous contribution to the hospital.
3. **Volition** – The power to make one's own choices or decisions.
    - Example: It was entirely her volition to leave the job and pursue a new career.
4. **Involuntary** – Done without conscious choice or control.
    - Example: The doctor explained that the muscle spasms were involuntary and beyond her control.

Language Time Travel: Volition and Volunteer

In Latin, the word **volitio** meant "a wish" or "will," evolving into "volition," which refers to the power of choosing. Over time, the meaning expanded to involve **voluntary** actions, and those who engage in them were termed **volunteers**. Historically, **volunteerism** was first seen as a self-chosen act of service, which is now central to many charitable causes worldwide.

Story: The Benevolent Volunteer

In a small town, there was a **voluntary** organization dedicated to helping those in need. The members worked tirelessly, driven by their own **volition** to make a difference. One day, a young woman named Clara, with a deep **benevolent** spirit, decided to join their cause. She wasn't asked or forced; it was simply her own **voluntary** choice to dedicate her time to a good cause.

Clara had always felt a strong desire to help others, and she was the first to sign up as a **volunteer** at the town's shelter. She believed that every act of kindness, no matter how small, had the power to change lives.

One afternoon, as she was preparing meals at the shelter, Clara remembered the moment she decided to volunteer. It was a choice she made of her own **volition**, and it filled her with purpose and joy. She realized that when people act out of **volition**, they give far more than just their time—they offer their hearts, their energy, and their commitment.

ROOT: "VI-" (MEANING: "LIFE")

The root **"vi-"** comes from the Latin word *vita*, meaning "life." It appears in words related to living, sustaining life, or something essential to life.

Vocabulary:
1. **Vital**: Essential or crucial to life or function.
    - Example: Water is vital for survival, as every living organism needs it to thrive.
2. **Revive**: To bring back to life or restore to health.
    - Example: The doctors worked hard to revive the patient after the accident.
3. **Survive**: To continue to live or exist, especially after difficult conditions.
    - Example: The family managed to survive the harsh winter in the mountains.
4. **Vitamin**: A natural substance found in food that is necessary for life and health.
    - Example: Eating a balanced diet ensures you get the necessary vitamins for strong immune health.

Word Duel: Vital vs. Optional
Question: Which word refers to something essential for life?
   A.) **Vital**
   B.) **Optional**

Correct Answer: Vital

Explanation: The word **vital** comes from the root "vi-" meaning "life," and refers to something that is absolutely necessary for life or survival. On the other hand, **optional** refers to something that is not essential and can be chosen or left out.

The Importance of Life

This list shows words related to the importance of life:
1. **Vital** – Absolutely necessary for life.
    - Example: A vital organ, like the heart, is crucial for survival.
2. **Revive** – To restore life or health to something that was nearly lost.
    - Example: The paramedics worked quickly to revive the unconscious man.
3. **Survive** – To endure and continue to live after hardship.
    - Example: The explorers had to survive a long, harsh winter in the frozen wilderness.
4. **Vitamin** – A substance essential for health and life.
    - Example: She takes a vitamin supplement every day to ensure she gets all the nutrients she needs.

Language Time Travel: Vi- and Vitality

The Latin word *vita* was the root for many terms related to life, like **vital** and **revive**, while **vitamin** is a more modern term derived from *vita* to describe essential nutrients that support health. The word **survive** also traces back to the Latin *supervivere*, meaning to live beyond or continue after adversity —reflecting life's resilience. Over time, these words have evolved to emphasize the importance of sustenance, health, and the energy required to live and thrive.

Story: The Vital Journey

On a quiet morning, Emma woke up feeling the weight of exhaustion. For the past week, she had been feeling unwell and had to **survive** through long days of fever and weakness. It felt like her energy was fading, and she was unsure how much longer she could keep going. But then, she remembered her grandmother's words: "If you want to **revive** your spirit and body, you must take care of your **vital** needs."

Determined to get better, Emma made a few changes to her diet. She started taking **vitamins** to boost her immune system and made sure to drink plenty of water. Slowly but surely, her energy began to return. She felt the difference each day as she became stronger, knowing that her body needed these **vital** resources to thrive.

ROOT: "FRIG-" (MEANING: "COLD")

The root **"frig-"** comes from the Latin word *frigus*, meaning "cold" or "chill." It appears in words related to low temperatures, coldness, or the process of cooling.

Vocabulary:
1. **Frigid**: Extremely cold or icy; lacking warmth, either physically or emotionally.
    - Example: The frigid winds made it impossible to go outside without a heavy coat.
2. **Refrigerate**: To cool or preserve food by lowering its temperature.
    - Example: You need to refrigerate the leftovers to keep them fresh for tomorrow.
3. **Frigidity**: The quality or state of being cold, either in temperature or in manner (emotionally cold).
    - Example: Her **frigidity** toward her colleagues made it difficult to work with her.
4. **Defrost**: To remove frost or ice from something by warming it.
    - Example: Be sure to **defrost** the chicken before you cook it, or it won't cook evenly.

Word Duel: Frigid vs. Warm
Question: Which word describes extremely cold

temperatures?

A.) Frigid
B.) Warm

Correct Answer: Frigid

Explanation: **Frigid** comes from the root "frig-" meaning "cold," and refers to extremely cold temperatures. **Warm**, on the other hand, describes a mild or comfortable heat.

Semantic Scale: From Cold to Warm

This scale shows words related to temperature, from cold to warm:

1. **Frigid** – Very cold, often to the point of discomfort.
   - Example: The frigid air made it hard to breathe outside.
2. **Refrigerate** – To cool or chill something, typically to preserve it.
   - Example: After cooking, refrigerate any leftovers immediately.
3. **Defrost** – To remove ice or frost, typically from food or an object.
   - Example: I need to **defrost** my car windows before I can drive.
4. **Warm** – Comfortable or moderate heat.
   - Example: The blanket kept me warm throughout the night.

Language Time Travel: Frig- and Freezing

The Latin word *frigus* meant "cold," and it is the root for many words that describe low temperatures. Over time, words like **frigid** and **refrigerate** evolved to refer to both the literal and metaphorical sense of coldness. **Defrost** emerged as a way to describe the process of returning something to a more usable state after being frozen, showing the connection between cold and warmth in everyday life.

Brief Story: The Frigid Morning

One early winter morning, Jake woke up to find the world outside covered in a thick layer of frost. The air was so

frigid that it almost hurt to breathe. He wrapped himself in a warm coat, but the **frigid** temperature made it difficult to feel comfortable.

As he made his way to the kitchen, Jake remembered that he had forgotten to **refrigerate** his leftover soup the night before. He quickly opened the fridge and realized it was still safe, though it needed to be **defrosted** before he could heat it again. He put the soup in the microwave and patiently waited for it to warm up.

Despite the **frigidity** outside, Jake felt a sense of relief and warmth as he sipped the hot soup, knowing the cold was no longer keeping him from his comfort.

ROOT: "FID-" (MEANING: "FAITH" OR "TRUST")

The root **"fid-"** comes from the Latin word *fides*, meaning "faith" or "trust." It appears in words related to belief, loyalty, or trustworthiness.

Vocabulary:
1. **Confidence**: A feeling of trust or belief in oneself or others.
    - Example: She approached the presentation with confidence, knowing she had prepared well.
2. **Infidelity**: The act of being unfaithful, especially in a relationship or marriage.
    - Example: His **infidelity** caused a deep rift in their marriage, and they struggled to rebuild trust.
3. **Fidelity**: Faithfulness or loyalty, especially in relationships or to a cause.
    - Example: The dog's **fidelity** to its owner was unmatched, always staying by his side no matter what.

Explanation: Confidence comes from the root "fid-" meaning "faith" and refers to a strong belief in one's abilities or in someone else's trustworthiness.

Semantic Scale: Levels of Trust
This scale shows words related to faith and trust:
1. **Confidence** – A feeling of belief or trust in oneself or others.
    - Example: She had enough **confidence** to lead the team with determination.
2. **Fidelity** – Loyalty and faithfulness, often in relationships.
    - Example: The couple's **fidelity** to one another was the foundation of their long-lasting marriage.
3. **Infidelity** – Disloyalty, often in romantic relationships.
    - Example: The **infidelity** was discovered when they found out he had been seeing someone else.

Language Time Travel: Fid- and Trust
The root **"fid-"** comes from *fides*, which means faith or trust in Latin. Over time, it evolved into many words that describe trust and loyalty, like **confidence, fidelity**, and **infidelity**. Words with this root reflect the essential role of trust in relationships, whether between people, institutions, or even oneself.

The Trust that Endures

Liam had always been a man of strong **confidence**. He believed in his ability to overcome any challenge, both in his career and his personal life. However, his trust in people was shaken when he learned of his close friend's **infidelity**—a betrayal that left him questioning what was real.

Despite the hurt, Liam found solace in the loyalty of his dog, who had always shown unwavering **fidelity**. The dog's loyalty reminded him that trust could still be found in the most unexpected places. It helped him slowly rebuild his belief in people.

ROOT: "DYNA-" (MEANING: "POWER")

The root **"dyna-"** originates from the Greek word *dynamis*, which means "power" or "strength." It appears in words related to force, energy, and strength, often conveying a sense of movement or change.

Vocabulary:
1. **Dynamic**: Describing something characterized by constant change, activity, or progress; energetic.
     - Example: Her **dynamic** personality always brought excitement to the team meetings.
2. **Dynasty**: A succession of rulers from the same family or line; a powerful family that maintains its influence over time.
     - Example: The Ming **dynasty** ruled China for over 300 years.
3. **Dynamite**: A powerful explosive material; something that has a significant, often explosive impact.
     - Example: The new marketing campaign was a **dynamite** success, boosting sales by 30%.
4. **Dynamism**: The quality of being full of energy, enthusiasm, and the drive for progress.
     - Example: The **dynamism** of the startup's leadership allowed them to disrupt the tech

industry.

Word Duel: Dynamic vs. Static
Question: Which word describes something full of energy and change?
   A.) Dynamic
   B.) Static
Correct Answer: Dynamic
Explanation: **Dynamic** comes from the root "dyna-" meaning "power" and is used to describe something that is constantly changing or full of energy. **Static**, on the other hand, refers to something that is unchanging or motionless, often lacking energy or movement.

Semantic Scale: From Powerlessness to Power
This scale shows words related to energy and force, ranging from low power to high power:
1. **Static** – Lack of motion or energy; still.
   - Example: The **static** atmosphere in the room made everyone feel uncomfortable.
2. **Dynamic** – Full of energy and change, with a sense of movement.
   - Example: Her **dynamic** leadership style helped transform the organization.
3. **Dynamism** – The driving force behind continuous change or energy.
   - Example: The **dynamism** of the economy created endless opportunities for growth.
4. **Dynamite** – A powerful explosive, often symbolizing forceful impact.
   - Example: The decision to cut costs was a **dynamite** move that saved the company millions.

Language Time Travel: Dyna- and Force
The Greek word *dynamis* gave rise to the root **"dyna-"**, which has been used in English to convey the idea of power, force, and change. Over time, words like **dynamic** and

dynamite have evolved, with **dynamic** describing energetic or changing entities, and **dynamite** symbolizing intense power or explosive impact. These words highlight how the concept of power has been used in various contexts, from human energy to destructive force.

Story: The Power of Change

In a small town, a young leader named Maya became the head of a local charity. Her **dynamic** approach to leadership immediately changed the atmosphere. Instead of maintaining the **static** structure that had existed for years, she encouraged new ideas and change, driving the team forward with her enthusiasm.

Under her leadership, the organization grew into something powerful, like a **dynasty** of positive change. Maya's relentless **dynamism** kept the team motivated, always striving for bigger goals. One year, she introduced a new fundraising event that was a **dynamite** success, raising enough money to expand the charity's reach into neighboring towns.

Maya's journey showed how **dynamic** leadership can transform an organization, just as a small spark can ignite a **dynamite** explosion, changing everything in its path.

ROOT: "VER-" (MEANING: "TRUE")

The root **"ver-"** originates from the Latin word *verus*, which means "true" or "genuine." It is used in words related to truth, authenticity, and accuracy. This root emphasizes reliability and the notion of what is correct or factual.

Vocabulary:
1. **Verify**: To confirm or make sure that something is true or accurate.
    - Example: Please **verify** the details on the form before submitting it.
2. **Veritable**: Genuine or real; used to emphasize the truth or authenticity of something.
    - Example: The ancient manuscript was a **veritable** treasure, offering insights into early civilizations.
3. **Verdict**: The decision or judgment made by a jury or judge in a court case, often referring to the truth of a matter.
    - Example: The jury delivered a **verdict** of guilty after a week-long trial.
4. **Veracity**: The quality of being truthful or accurate; devotion to the truth.
    - Example: The journalist was known for her **veracity**, always ensuring the facts were

correct.

Word Duel: Verify vs. Deny

Question: Which word means to confirm something as true?
 A.) Verify
 B.) Deny

Correct Answer: Verify

Explanation: **Verify** comes from the root "ver-" meaning "true," and it means to confirm or check something's truthfulness or accuracy. **Deny** means to reject or declare something untrue.

Semantic Scale: Levels of Truth

This scale shows words related to truth, ranging from mild uncertainty to full certainty:

 1. **False** – Not true; incorrect or deceptive.
 Example: The news report was based on **false** information, which was later corrected.

 2. **Doubtful** – Uncertain, not fully true or confirmed.
 Example: His story seemed **doubtful** given the lack of evidence.

 3. **Verify** – To check or confirm that something is true.
 Example: Before making a decision, I need to **verify** the facts.

 4. **True** – In accordance with facts or reality.
 Example: The detective found the **true** story behind the mysterious disappearance.

 5. **Verifiable** – Able to be proven true through evidence.
 Example: The scientist's claims were **verifiable** through experiments and observations.

 6. **Veracity** – The quality of being truthful or accurate.
 Example: The lawyer's **veracity** in presenting the case impressed the jury.

Language Time Travel: Ver- and Truth

The root **"ver-"** comes from the Latin *verus*, meaning "true" or "genuine." Words like **verify, verifiable,** and **veracity** evolved from this root to emphasize the importance of confirming truth and accuracy. **Verdict** also stems from the Latin word *verus*, highlighting the role of truth in legal judgment. Over time, this root has come to represent the search for and confirmation of truth in various fields, from science to law to everyday life.

Story: The Power of Truth

Sarah was a journalist known for her **veracity** in reporting. She always took the time to **verify** every detail before publishing, ensuring that the news she shared with her readers was based on solid, **verifiable** facts. One day, she came across a story about a famous local artist, but the initial information seemed **doubtful**.

Determined to uncover the **true** story, Sarah conducted interviews and gathered documents to confirm the facts. After a thorough investigation, she was able to **verify** the artist's past, proving that his work had been inspired by his experiences during a difficult time in his life. Her article was met with praise for its depth and accuracy.

In the end, Sarah's commitment to the **veritable** truth helped restore trust in her reporting, reinforcing the importance of **veracity** in journalism. The **verdict** of her hard work was clear: truth always prevails.

ROOT: "LUC-" (MEANING: "LIGHT")

The root **"luc-"** comes from the Latin word *lux*, meaning "light." This root is used in words related to clarity, brightness, and the ability to see or understand. **Luc-** is associated with anything that helps to shed light, both literally and figuratively.

Vocabulary:
1. **Illuminate**: To light up or make something brighter, often to clarify or explain something.
    - Example: The professor's explanation helped **illuminate** the complex topic for the students.
2. **Lucid**: Clear and easy to understand; often used to describe clear thought or writing.
    - Example: His **lucid** explanation of the theory made it accessible to everyone.
3. **Translucent**: Allowing light to pass through, but not transparent; semi-transparent.
    - Example: The **translucent** curtains let in just enough light to brighten the room without being too bright.
4. **Luminous**: Emitting light, especially in the dark; bright or radiant.
    - Example: The stars were **luminous** against

the night sky, creating a breathtaking view.

Word Duel: Lucid vs. Obscure

Question: Which word refers to something that is clear and easily understood?

   A.) Lucid
   B.) Obscure

Correct Answer: Lucid

Explanation: **Lucid** comes from the root **"luc-"**, meaning "light," and refers to something that is clear, easily understood, or shining with clarity. **Obscure**, on the other hand, means unclear or hard to understand.

Semantic Scale: Levels of Clarity

This scale shows words related to clarity, from complete obscurity to full understanding:

1. **Opaque** – Not letting light through; completely unclear.
    - Example: The **opaque** glass made it difficult to see what was inside the box.
2. **Obscure** – Not clear or hard to understand.
    - Example: The article was **obscure** and left many readers confused.
3. **Translucent** – Allowing some light to pass through; somewhat clear.
    - Example: The **translucent** paper made the image slightly visible but not fully detailed.
4. **Lucid** – Clear and easy to understand.
    - Example: After the explanation, the instructions seemed **lucid** and straightforward.
5. **Luminous** – Shining brightly, often with an inner light.
    - Example: The **luminous** moon lit up the night sky, casting a soft glow on the landscape.

Language Time Travel: Luc- and Light

The root **"luc-"** originates from the Latin *lux*, meaning "light." Words like **illuminate** and **lucid** have evolved from this root to convey the ideas of making something visible or clear. **Luminous**, often used to describe things that glow or shine, comes from the same root and emphasizes the power of light to guide or clarify. Over time, the connection between light and clarity has extended beyond the literal sense to include mental and emotional clarity, as seen in words like **lucid**.

Story: The Power of Light

At the beginning of her career, Maya struggled to understand the complexities of molecular biology. Her textbook was dense, full of **obscure** language that made the subject feel impossible to grasp. However, after meeting Dr. Collins, a renowned professor, her entire perspective changed.

Dr. Collins had the ability to **illuminate** any concept. Her teaching was always **lucid**, and no matter how complex the topic, Maya felt it was within her reach. One day, while reading a chapter on cellular processes, Maya stumbled upon a particularly tricky passage. However, with Dr. Collins' help, the explanation became as **luminous** as the light breaking through a dark cloud. The dense material became **translucent**—still complicated but now just clear enough to understand.

As Maya's understanding deepened, she realized that the true value of **lucid** teaching was not only in making difficult subjects easier to grasp, but in fostering a lifelong love of learning.

ROOT: "CENT-" (MEANING: "HUNDRED")

The root **"cent-"** comes from the Latin word *centum*, meaning "hundred." It is commonly used in words referring to numbers, quantities, and intervals related to "one hundred" or a portion of a hundred.

Vocabulary:
1. **Century**: A period of 100 years or the number 100.
    - Example: The United States will celebrate its **century** of independence in 2076.
2. **Centimeter**: A unit of measurement equal to one-hundredth of a meter.
    - Example: The paper was only 2 **centimeters** thick, making it very lightweight.
3. **Percent**: A way of expressing a number as a fraction of 100, often used to describe proportions.
    - Example: The company saw a **percent** increase in sales after launching the new product.
4. **Centennial**: A 100th anniversary or celebration of a 100-year period.
    - Example: The city is planning a grand parade for its **centennial** celebration in 2024.

Word Duel: Percent vs. Decimal
Question: Which term represents a fraction of 100 in a more

commonly used format?
   A.) Percent
   B.) Decimal

Correct Answer: Percent

Explanation: **Percent** comes from the root **"cent-"**, meaning "hundred," and represents a number out of 100. It is commonly used to show proportions, such as in statistics or finances. A **decimal** expresses a fraction but not specifically out of 100, and is used in different contexts.

Semantic Scale: Values

This scale shows words related to percentages, from complete lack to full presence:

1. **Zero** – No amount or presence.
   - Example: The company had **zero** growth last quarter.
2. **Few** – A small amount, not reaching 10%.
   - Example: Only a **few** students passed the exam.
3. **Some** – A moderate amount, more than a few but less than half.
   - Example: **Some** participants enjoyed the new feature, but not all.
4. **Most** – More than 70%, a large majority.
   - Example: **Most** of the team supported the new project plan.
5. **Hundred Percent** – The entirety or complete amount.
   - Example: He was **hundred percent** committed to the project.

Language Time Travel: Cent- and Its Influence

The root **"cent-"** traces back to the Latin *centum*, meaning "hundred." The word **century** originally referred to a group of one hundred soldiers in ancient Rome, but over time, it came to mean a 100-year period. **Centimeter** and **percent** are both direct descendants of **centum**, and they retain the idea of dividing something into 100 parts, whether it be in measurements or proportions. The use of **centennial** celebrates a significant milestone reached after 100 years, keeping the connection to the root intact in modern usage.

Story: The Hundred-Year Journey

In 1924, the city of Riverton was founded. It began as a small village with just a handful of families, but over the next **century**, it grew into a bustling metropolitan area. By 2024, the city was preparing for its **centennial** celebration, marking 100 years since its founding.

During the preparations, city officials conducted surveys to find out what percentage of residents were excited about the event. They discovered that **sixty percent** of the population was eager to participate, while the remaining **forty percent** were indifferent. The mayor, however, was **hundred percent** committed to making the centennial celebration the most memorable event in the city's history.

As the big day approached, the town center was transformed, and everyone—no matter their **centimeter** of space—was thrilled to be part of the grand occasion. The centennial celebration was not just a moment to look back on the past, but to look forward to the next **century** of growth and opportunity for Riverton.

ROOT: "DOX-" (MEANING: "OPINION" OR "BELIEF")

The root **"dox-"** comes from the Greek word *doxa*, meaning "opinion" or "belief." It is often used in words that relate to different types of belief systems or contradictory ideas, and it forms the foundation for terms in philosophy, religion, and logic.

Vocabulary:
1. **Orthodox**: Adhering to established or traditional beliefs, especially in religion.
    - Example: The church followed the **orthodox** teachings, maintaining long-established practices.
2. **Heterodox**: Differing from or contrary to established beliefs or opinions.
    - Example: The professor's **heterodox** views on economics challenged traditional theories.
3. **Paradox**: A statement that appears contradictory or self-refuting but may reveal a deeper truth.
    - Example: The statement "less is more" is a **paradox**, as it contradicts itself but often holds true in certain contexts.

4. **Doxology**: A short hymn or expression of praise to God, typically used in Christian worship.
     - Example: The congregation sang a **doxology** at the end of the service, praising the divine.

Word Duel: Orthodox vs. Heterodox
Question: Which word refers to holding traditional or accepted beliefs?
   A.) Orthodox
   B.) Heterodox
Correct Answer: Orthodox
Explanation: **Orthodox** comes from the Greek *orthos* (correct) and *doxa* (opinion), meaning "correct opinion," and it refers to adhering to accepted standards, particularly in religion or philosophy. **Heterodox**, on the other hand, comes from *heteros* (other) and *doxa*, meaning "other opinion," and is used to describe beliefs that are outside the conventional or accepted norms.

Semantic Scale: Belief Systems
This scale shows words related to different types of belief, from traditional to controversial:
1. **Orthodox** – Conforming to established beliefs.
     - Example: The **orthodox** church follows traditional teachings.
2. **Conventional** – Following widely accepted beliefs, though not necessarily the oldest.
     - Example: His views on social issues were conventional but not extreme.
3. **Heterodox** – Diverging from the accepted beliefs.
     - Example: The scientist's **heterodox** theories were met with skepticism.
4. **Radical** – Completely differing from the established belief system.
     - Example: The activist pushed for **radical** change in society's structure.
5. **Paradoxical** – A belief that seems contradictory yet

may be true.
- Example: The idea that **paradoxical** thinking can sometimes reveal deeper truths is widely acknowledged in philosophy.

Language Time Travel: Dox- and its Evolution

The Greek root **"doxa"** meant "opinion" or "belief." In ancient Greece, the term was used to describe various types of opinion—whether true, false, or subjective. The term **orthodox** evolved to specifically mean "correct opinion" and was used to describe conformity to established religious or philosophical doctrines. Over time, **heterodox** came to refer to ideas that were contrary to the mainstream or accepted ones. **Paradox**, on the other hand, originated as a rhetorical device, signifying a statement that contradicts itself yet might hold a hidden truth. Today, all these words serve to highlight how beliefs, both accepted and unconventional, shape our understanding of the world.

Story: The Paradox of Belief

In a quiet village, there were two schools of thought. The **orthodox** villagers followed the old ways, believing that their ancestors' teachings were the only true path. They lived simple lives, believing that stability was the key to happiness. Meanwhile, a **heterodox** philosopher came to the village, offering radical new ideas. He argued that progress could only come through challenging traditional beliefs. His **paradoxical** statements, such as "to gain, you must first lose," puzzled many.

Despite the initial skepticism, some villagers began to question the old ways. They found that by accepting the **heterodox** ideas, they could improve their lives in ways they never thought possible. Others, however, remained steadfast in their **orthodox** beliefs, unwilling to accept change. In the village's center, a small group of people gathered every Sunday to sing the **doxology**, praising the divine for giving them the wisdom to navigate both new and old beliefs.

In this story, the words **orthodox**, **heterodox**, **paradox**, and **doxology** reflect the complex journey of belief—how ideas can either bind us to the past or propel us forward into new understandings.

ROOT: "AGRI-" (MEANING: "FIELD" OR "FARM")

The root **"agri-"** comes from the Latin *ager*, meaning "field" or "farm." This root is used in words that relate to farming, land cultivation, and the study or business of agriculture. It reflects the close connection between human societies and the land they work on for sustenance and livelihood.

Vocabulary:
1. **Agriculture**: The practice of cultivating soil, growing crops, and raising animals for food, fiber, and other products.
    - Example: **Agriculture** has been the backbone of human civilization for thousands of years.
2. **Agrarian**: Related to land, farming, or rural matters; often used to describe a society or economy that is based on agriculture.
    - Example: The country had an **agrarian** economy, with most people working on farms.
3. **Agronomy**: The science of soil management and crop production.
    - Example: **Agronomy** has evolved to include modern technologies like genetically modified crops and irrigation systems.
4. **Agribusiness**: The business and commercial aspect

of agriculture, involving the production, processing, and distribution of agricultural products.
- Example: **Agribusiness** has become a global industry, with large corporations dominating food production and distribution.

Word Duel: Agriculture vs. Agribusiness

Question: Which term refers to the science and practice of farming, including growing crops and raising animals?

A.) Agriculture
B.) Agribusiness

Correct Answer: Agriculture

Explanation: **Agriculture** refers to the broad practice and study of farming, which includes crop production, soil management, and livestock raising. **Agribusiness**, however, focuses on the commercial side of agriculture, including the business practices, production, and distribution processes related to farming.

Land Use and Economy

This list shows words related to land use, from traditional farming to industrialized agriculture:

1. **Agriculture** – The practice of growing crops and raising animals for food, fiber, and resources.
   - Example: The country thrives due to its focus on **agriculture**.
2. **Agrarian** – Pertaining to farming and the land, often used to describe societies or economies based on farming.
   - Example: In an **agrarian** society, most people live in rural areas and work the land.
3. **Agronomy** – The science and technology of soil management and crop production.
   - Example: **Agronomy** involves research into sustainable farming techniques and crop yields.

4. **Agribusiness** – The business side of agriculture, which includes the commercial aspects of farming such as processing, packaging, and selling crops and livestock.
    - Example: Large **agribusiness** corporations control much of the global food market.

Language Time Travel: Agriculture and its Evolution

The word **agriculture** has its roots in Latin *ager* meaning "field" and *cultura*, meaning "cultivation." Agriculture has been the foundation of human civilization, starting with early societies learning to cultivate crops and domesticate animals. Over time, the focus shifted from basic survival to the development of complex farming techniques, including crop rotation, irrigation, and the use of fertilizers.

As society advanced, so did the business side of farming, leading to the rise of **agribusiness** in the 20th century. This term emerged as farming became more industrialized, with large-scale production and commercialization driving the food industry on a global scale. The field of **agronomy** grew in response to the need for scientific methods to improve farming productivity and sustainability.

Story: The Evolution of Agriculture

Long ago, in a small village nestled between fertile fields, people worked the land. Their lives revolved around **agriculture**, as they grew enough crops to sustain themselves. Over time, the village's economy shifted, and the town became more **agrarian**, with everyone depending on the land for their livelihood.

As the village grew, it attracted scientists and innovators who studied **agronomy**, seeking ways to improve crop yields and manage the soil more effectively. With the advent of modern technology, farming methods changed drastically. A local farm, once small and independent, grew into a massive **agribusiness**, supplying food to cities far and wide.

Through these changes, the villagers realized that **agriculture** had evolved from simple farming into a complex, science-driven business. Yet, the foundation of their society remained grounded in the same soil that had sustained them for generations.

ROOT: "SOL-" (MEANING: "ALONE" OR "SUN")

The root **"sol-"** has two main meanings. In one context, it refers to the **sun**, derived from the Latin *sol*, meaning "sun." In another, it refers to **being alone**, derived from the Latin *solus*, meaning "alone" or "only." This root is reflected in words related to isolation, the sun, and things that are singular or unique.

Vocabulary:
1. **Solitary**: Existing or living alone; without others.
    - Example: After a long day at work, he enjoyed the peace of his **solitary** walk in the park.
2. **Solitude**: The state of being alone or isolated from others, often by choice.
    - Example: She embraced the **solitude** of the mountain cabin, finding peace in her own company.
3. **Solar**: Relating to the sun, or powered by the sun's energy.
    - Example: The house was equipped with **solar** panels to harness energy from the sun.
4. **Desolate**: A place that is deserted, empty, or lacking in life; often evokes feelings of loneliness.
    - Example: The **desolate** landscape stretched

for miles, with not a single building in sight.

Word Duel: Solitary vs. Social

Question: Which word describes someone who prefers to be alone or in isolation?

    A.) Solitary
    B.) Social

Correct Answer: Solitary

Explanation: **Solitary** refers to the state of being alone, often by choice. A **solitary** person enjoys or is comfortable with isolation. In contrast, a **social** person thrives in the company of others, enjoying interaction and connection.

Semantic Scale: Aloneness and Loneliness

This scale shows different levels of isolation, from peaceful solitude to emptiness:

1. **Solitary** – Existing alone, often by choice, without company or companionship.
    - Example: She took a **solitary** trip to the mountains for some time to reflect.
2. **Solitude** – The state of being alone, especially in a peaceful or quiet setting.
    - Example: He cherished the **solitude** of his cabin in the woods, where he could focus on writing.
3. **Desolate** – A place or state of extreme emptiness, often evoking sadness or loneliness.
    - Example: The once bustling town had turned **desolate**, with buildings crumbling and no one in sight.

Language Time Travel: Solitude and Solar

The roots **sol-** for "alone" and "sun" have their origins in Latin. *Solus* (meaning "alone") is the root for words like **solitary** and **solitude**, while *sol* (meaning "sun") is the origin of **solar** and **solstice**. These two meanings of **sol-** have remained distinct but both carry a sense of singularity—whether it is the solitary existence of a person or the sun as a unique celestial body in our sky.

The word **solar** comes from the Latin *solaris*, meaning "of the sun," while **solitude** comes from *solitudo*, meaning "the state of being alone." As people began to recognize the vastness of the sun's importance in daily life and growth, they also began to understand the psychological and emotional benefits of **solitude**.

Story: The Solitude of the Desert

In the heart of the vast desert, Elena ventured out into the **solitary** stretch of land, leaving behind the noise and chaos of the city. The **solitude** she found in the desert was peaceful, allowing her to reflect deeply on her life. The sun blazed overhead, its **solar** rays beating down on the sand, creating an almost otherworldly atmosphere.

Though the landscape was beautiful, there was also a sense of **desolation**. The once lively desert had now become empty, its vast stretches feeling isolated and forlorn. Yet, Elena didn't mind. She embraced this feeling of being alone, finding a kind of clarity in the quiet. The warmth of the sun was all she needed as she walked through the barren yet beautiful wilderness, finding solace in her **solitary** journey.

ROOT: "VIRT-" (MEANING: "STRENGTH" OR "POWER")

The root **"virt-"** comes from the Latin word *virtus*, meaning "strength" or "power," especially in a moral or personal sense. Over time, this root has evolved to also represent qualities such as skill, excellence, and moral goodness. It appears in words that convey not only physical strength but also inner strength, integrity, and high quality.

Vocabulary:
1. **Virtue**: A moral excellence, goodness, or righteousness.
    - Example: Honesty is considered a **virtue** that leads to trust and respect in relationships.
2. **Virtuoso**: A person highly skilled in a particular art, especially music or the fine arts.
    - Example: The **virtuoso** pianist captivated the audience with his flawless performance.
3. **Virtual**: Existing in essence or effect, though not physically present, often used in the context of digital spaces.
    - Example: With the rise of technology, many meetings have gone **virtual**, conducted

entirely online.
4. **Virtuous**: Having or showing high moral standards; morally good or righteous.
    - Example: She led a **virtuous** life, always acting with kindness and honesty.

Word Duel: Virtuous vs. Vicious
Question: Which word describes someone with excellent moral character?
   A.) Virtuous
   B.) Vicious
Correct Answer: Virtuous
Explanation: **Virtuous** describes a person with high moral character, who embodies qualities such as kindness, honesty, and integrity. **Vicious**, on the other hand, refers to someone or something characterized by cruelty or immoral behavior, making the two words opposites.

Moral Qualities
This list shows words related to virtue, ranging from moderate to extreme levels of moral excellence or strength:
1. **Virtuous** – A person who consistently exhibits good moral qualities.
    - Example: The **virtuous** leader was admired for her unwavering commitment to justice and fairness.
2. **Virtue** – The quality of having high moral standards or excellence in character.
    - Example: Patience is a **virtue** that is often tested in difficult situations.
3. **Virtuoso** – A person who excels in a particular skill, often in the arts or music.
    - Example: The **virtuoso** violinist amazed the audience with his technical prowess and emotional depth.
4. **Virtual** – Referring to something that exists in essence or effect, though not physically present, such

as a virtual meeting or a virtual reality experience.
- Example: Many **virtual** platforms offer opportunities for people to connect and work together online.

Language Time Travel: Virtue and Virtuoso

The word **virtue** comes from the Latin *virtus*, which meant moral strength and excellence. Over time, the term expanded to include physical strength and skill. **Virtuoso** evolved from this root but focuses more on technical skill, particularly in music and the arts, describing a person with exceptional mastery.

The concept of **virtue** originally emphasized inner strength and moral integrity, while a **virtuoso** was someone who demonstrated excellence in a specific domain. In both cases, **virt-** emphasizes an exceptional level of power, whether in moral strength or specialized skill.

Story: The Virtuoso's Virtue

In a small town nestled in the hills, there lived a **virtuoso** violinist named Lucas. He had spent years perfecting his craft, earning respect and admiration for his skill. But what set him apart wasn't just his musical talent; it was his **virtue**—the way he lived his life with kindness, humility, and generosity.

Lucas was known not only for his flawless performances but also for his willingness to help others. He often held free lessons for young, aspiring musicians, encouraging them to follow their passion with the same dedication that he had.

One day, a traveler came to town and watched Lucas perform. After the performance, he told Lucas, "You are a **virtuoso**, not only in music but in life. Your **virtue** shines brighter than your violin."

Lucas smiled humbly, knowing that true greatness lies not just in talent but in the strength of character. And it was this **virtue** that made his music resonate deeply with everyone who heard it.

ROOT: "LUN-" (MEANING: "MOON")

The root **"lun-"** comes from the Latin word *luna*, meaning "moon." This root has inspired a range of words associated with the moon, its phases, and things connected to its mysterious or sometimes unpredictable influence. The term is often used to describe anything that is moon-related, or metaphorically, to describe behavior or phenomena influenced by the moon.

Vocabulary:
1. **Lunar**: Relating to the moon.
    - Example: The **lunar** eclipse captivated everyone, as the moon darkened for several minutes.
2. **Lunatic**: An outdated and offensive term once used to describe someone who was mentally ill, believed to be affected by the phases of the moon. Now used more figuratively for someone acting irrationally.
    - Example: His sudden outburst made everyone think he had gone **lunatic**, though they knew it was just the stress getting to him.
3. **Interlude**: A pause or break in between parts of something, originally referring to a musical

or dramatic performance between acts or scenes, metaphorically tied to the idea of a "break" like the moon's phases.
- Example: The **interlude** in the concert provided a brief, soothing respite before the final act.

4. **Lunisolar**: Pertaining to both the moon and the sun, often used to describe systems that are influenced by both celestial bodies, such as certain calendars.
   - Example: The **lunisolar** calendar accounts for both the moon's phases and the sun's cycle.

Word Duel: Lunar vs. Lunatic

Question: Which word describes something related to the moon?

A.) Lunar
B.) Lunatic

Correct Answer: Lunar

Explanation: **Lunar** refers to anything related to the moon, such as a **lunar** eclipse or **lunar** landscape. **Lunatic**, on the other hand, is an outdated term historically linked to moon phases, but now used to describe irrational or crazy behavior, often in a metaphorical sense.

Semantic Scale: Phases of the Moon

This scale shows words related to the moon, from literal to metaphorical connections:

1. **Lunar** – Directly relating to the moon.
   - Example: Astronauts studied **lunar** soil samples during their mission.
2. **Lunisolar** – Pertaining to both the moon and the sun.
   - Example: The **lunisolar** calendar was used by ancient civilizations to predict seasonal changes.
3. **Interlude** – A break or pause in something, originally connected to performances or phases in time.

- Example: The play featured a brief **interlude** between the two acts.
4. **Lunatic** – Originally linked to the belief that the moon could cause mental instability, now used metaphorically for erratic behavior.
    - Example: She dismissed the **lunatic** rumors about the storm, understanding it was simply a strong wind.

Language Time Travel: Lunar and Lunatic
In ancient times, people believed that the moon had a direct effect on human behavior, especially in influencing mood swings and mental states. This belief gave rise to the word **lunatic**, which was used to describe people whose behavior was thought to be influenced by the phases of the moon. The term **lunar**, on the other hand, simply refers to anything associated with the moon, such as **lunar** cycles or **lunar** exploration.
Though the term **lunatic** is now considered outdated and offensive, the **lunar** root still remains widely used in scientific contexts, such as the study of the moon and its impact on the Earth.

Story: The Lunar Festival
In the small village of Everwood, the people eagerly awaited the annual **lunar** festival, a celebration of the full moon. It was said that on this night, the moon's glow would shine brighter than ever, bringing a sense of peace to all. The village was also famous for its **lunisolar** calendar, which carefully tracked both the moon's phases and the sun's path, helping farmers determine the perfect time for planting crops.

This year, however, a strange event occurred. As the **lunar** eclipse began, a local man named Jack, known for his unpredictable behavior, started acting unusually. The villagers whispered that the eclipse had turned him into a **lunatic**, but his friends, knowing him well, just laughed it off, recognizing his outbursts as nothing more than a prank.

As the **interlude** of the eclipse passed, the moon returned to its normal phase, and Jack calmed down, enjoying the rest of the festivities with the others. The festival continued under the soft glow of the moon, and all was well again in Everwood.

ROOT: "CHRONO-" (MEANING: "TIME")

The root **"chrono-"** comes from the Greek word *chronos*, meaning "time." This root is used in words related to the concept of time, whether in measuring it, organizing it, or describing things that happen over a period of time. Many of the words derived from **chrono-** deal with the way time is experienced, measured, or conceptualized.

Vocabulary:
1. **Chronology**: The arrangement of events in the order of their occurrence.
    - Example: The historian created a **chronology** of ancient Rome to trace its rise and fall over centuries.
2. **Synchronize**: To cause events or actions to happen at the same time.
    - Example: The dancers practiced for weeks to **synchronize** their movements perfectly for the performance.
3. **Chronic**: Describes something that lasts for a long time or recurs frequently, especially with illnesses or conditions.
    - Example: He suffered from **chronic** back pain, which made everyday activities difficult.

4. **Chronometer**: An instrument used for measuring time, especially accurately.
    - Example: Sailors rely on a **chronometer** to calculate their longitude at sea.

Word Duel: Chronology vs. Chronic
Question: Which word refers to something happening over a long period of time?
   A.) Chronology
   B.) Chronic

Correct Answer: **Chronic**
Explanation: **Chronic** describes something, often a condition or illness, that continues or recurs over a long period of time. **Chronology**, on the other hand, refers to the ordering of events according to time, not the duration of time itself.

Time-Related Concepts
This list shows words ranging from precise time measurement to ongoing time-related experiences:
1. **Chronometer** – A device used for precise time measurement.
    - Example: The **chronometer** helped them measure time accurately on their long voyage.
2. **Synchronize** – To make things happen at the same time.
    - Example: The team worked hard to **synchronize** their watches for the experiment.
3. **Chronology** – The sequence of events in time.
    - Example: The **chronology** of the space mission was carefully recorded.
4. **Chronic** – A long-lasting or recurring condition.
    - Example: He lived with **chronic** fatigue for many years before receiving a diagnosis.

Language Time Travel: Chronos and Chronology

The word **chrono-** comes from the Greek god **Chronos**, who was said to personify time. In ancient myth, Chronos was often depicted as an all-powerful force that controlled the passing of time. Over time, **chrono-** evolved into a root used to refer to anything related to time, from the study of historical sequences (chronology) to the precise measurement of time (chronometer). The word **chronic**, for instance, reflects time's persistent nature, as something that continues for a long period.

Story: The Timekeeper's Legacy

In the quiet town of Timelake, the village historian, Mr. Thorne, spent years researching the **chronology** of the town's founding, carefully tracing the events that led to its establishment. Every year, the town would celebrate the anniversary of its founding, and the elders would share stories about the early settlers.

On the night of the anniversary, the village's clock tower, a magnificent **chronometer**, chimed as it had for centuries, marking the passage of another year. However, during the celebration, an unfortunate event occurred: a local artist, known for his unbreakable focus, began to feel the effects of **chronic** fatigue. He had spent countless hours working on a mural for the event, and the exhaustion finally took its toll.

The villagers, understanding that the artist needed rest, decided to **synchronize** their efforts to ensure he would have the time he needed to recover. They postponed some of the evening's events to give him space. The town continued to celebrate, not just the passage of time but the importance of balancing the moments in life.

The **chronology** of Timelake's founding, the **chronometer** marking each year, and the story of the artist's recovery all reflected how time—whether precise or ongoing—shapes their community and lives.

ROOT: "VOLV-" (MEANING: "ROLL" OR "TURN")

The root **"volv-"** comes from the Latin verb *volvĕre*, meaning "to roll" or "to turn." This root is seen in words that involve the idea of rolling, turning, or changing shape or direction. These words often convey a sense of movement, progression, or circularity.

Vocabulary:
1. **Revolve**: To move in a circular or curved path around something.
    - Example: The planets **revolve** around the sun in a precise orbit.
2. **Evolution**: The gradual development of something, especially from a simple to a more complex form.
    - Example: Darwin's theory of **evolution** revolutionized our understanding of biology.
3. **Involve**: To include or make a part of a situation, activity, or process.
    - Example: The project will **involve** several teams working together over the next few months.
4. **Convoluted**: Extremely complex and difficult to follow or understand, often involving many twists and turns.

- Example: The detective struggled to make sense of the **convoluted** mystery, filled with unexpected twists.

Word Duel: Involve vs. Evolve

Question: Which word refers to something changing or developing over time?
- A.) Involve
- B.) Evolve

Correct Answer: **Evolve**

Explanation: **Evolve** comes from the root **"volv-"** and refers to gradual development or change, often implying progress or transformation over time. **Involve**, on the other hand, means to include someone or something in an activity or situation.

Semantic Scale: Levels of Movement

This scale shows words related to movement, from straightforward rotation to complex development:

1. **Revolve** – To move in a circular motion around an axis.
    - Example: The **revolutions** of the Earth create the cycle of days and nights.
2. **Evolve** – To change or develop gradually, often for the better.
    - Example: Over millions of years, species **evolved** to adapt to their environments.
3. **Involve** – To include or engage someone or something in a process or situation.
    - Example: The new system will **involve** the cooperation of all departments.
4. **Convoluted** – Highly complex, often to the point of being difficult to understand.
    - Example: The **convoluted** instructions confused everyone at the start.

Language Time Travel: Evolution of "Volv-"

The root **"volv-"** comes from the Latin verb *volvěre*, meaning "to roll." This concept of rolling or turning was extended metaphorically to ideas of continuous movement, change, and development. Over time, words like **evolve** and **revolve** emerged, carrying this sense of gradual motion, whether it was the rotation of celestial bodies or the slow process of natural development. The idea of things rolling forward or evolving became central to both the physical and conceptual growth in language.

Story: The Evolution of the Village

In a small village nestled between hills, the townspeople would gather every year to celebrate the progress their community had made. The village had **evolved** from a small settlement into a thriving hub of commerce and culture. Every year, they would **revolve** around the central plaza, where a large, ancient tree stood at the heart of the town. The tree had witnessed many changes over the centuries, just as the village had.

One year, a new road was built that would **involve** even more people from outside the village in their growing business. While this was a great advancement, it came with challenges. The newcomers brought different ideas and technologies that, at times, seemed **convoluted** to the village elders who were used to their old ways. Despite the complexity of this change, the villagers saw it as part of their continuous **evolution**—a symbol of how their community, like the turning of a wheel, must keep moving forward, no matter how complex the journey might become.

As they looked toward the future, they knew that the cycle of progress would always **revolve**, bringing new challenges and opportunities in their path.

ROOT: "INTER-" (MEANING: "BETWEEN" OR "AMONG")

The root **"inter-"** comes from the Latin *inter*, meaning "between" or "among." This root is used in words that suggest an interaction or relationship involving more than one thing, group, or entity. It conveys a sense of connection or action that happens between two or more points.

Vocabulary:
1. **International**: Between or among nations; involving more than one country.
    - Example: The **international** conference brought together experts from around the world to discuss climate change.
2. **Interaction**: The action or influence between two or more people or things.
    - Example: The **interaction** between the teacher and students was lively and engaging during the lesson.
3. **Intervene**: To come between or take action to alter the course of an event.
    - Example: The doctor had to **intervene** to stop the bleeding after the injury.
4. **Intercept**: To stop or seize something before it

reaches its destination, often between two points.
- Example: The security team managed to **intercept** the package before it left the building.

Word Duel: Intervene vs. Intercept
Question: Which word involves stopping or interrupting something before it continues?
A.) Intervene
B.) Intercept

Correct Answer: Intercept
Explanation: **Intercept** means to stop something from continuing, usually before it reaches its intended destination (e.g., intercepting a letter, or a ball in sports). **Intervene** means to get involved in a situation, often to alter the outcome, but not necessarily to stop something before it continues.

Levels of Involvement Between Entities
This list shows the increasing degree of interaction between entities, from basic communication to more direct action:

1. **Interact** – To engage in reciprocal action, usually in communication.
   - Example: The two speakers **interacted** during the panel discussion, exchanging ideas.
2. **Intervene** – To come between or become involved in order to change or influence something.
   - Example: The counselor decided to **intervene** in the dispute to help resolve the issue.
3. **Intercept** – To stop something from continuing before it reaches its target.
   - Example: The police were able to **intercept** the shipment of illegal goods.
4. **International** – Involving multiple countries or crossing national boundaries.

- Example: The **international** summit focused on global environmental issues.

Language Time Travel: The Evolution of "Inter-"

The prefix **"inter-"** originates from the Latin *inter*, meaning "between" or "among." It has been used for centuries to describe actions, processes, or relationships that involve two or more parties. Over time, **"inter-"** became essential for conveying ideas of connection or interaction, not just in physical spaces, but also in the conceptual or social spheres. For example, the word **international** arose to describe relations or activities involving multiple countries. Similarly, **intervene** and **intercept** evolved to describe actions that occur between two points, such as people or objects, highlighting a crucial moment of interaction or interference.

Story: The International Peace Agreement

In the early 20th century, countries around the world had been in constant conflict, with few opportunities for peaceful **interaction**. Amidst the chaos, diplomats from various nations decided to **intervene** to negotiate a peace agreement. These leaders realized that in order to avoid further war, they needed to **intercept** hostile actions before they escalated into violence. Their efforts led to the formation of an **international** organization designed to promote diplomacy and prevent conflict.

However, during the negotiations, one country tried to sabotage the talks. The peacekeepers acted quickly to **intercept** any attempts to derail the process. As a result, they successfully **intervened**, and the peace agreement was signed. The event was celebrated as a victory for global cooperation, with the agreement symbolizing the power of nations coming together for the greater good. The world had seen the fruits of **international** collaboration, demonstrating that when people work together **among** each other, great things can be achieved.

ROOT: "ASTER-" (MEANING: "STAR")

The root **"aster-"** originates from the Greek word *astron*, meaning "star." This root is commonly found in words that relate to stars or celestial bodies, as well as in terms that metaphorically reference something that is bright or important. It is a key root in fields like astronomy, as well as in expressions of prominence or significance.

Vocabulary:
1. **Astronomy**: The scientific study of celestial bodies, such as stars, planets, and galaxies.
    - Example: **Astronomy** has fascinated humans for centuries, from ancient stargazing to modern space exploration.
2. **Asteroid**: A small rocky body that orbits the sun, often in the asteroid belt between Mars and Jupiter.
    - Example: The **asteroid** passed close to Earth, causing a brief moment of excitement among scientists and stargazers.
3. **Asterisk**: A symbol (*) used in text to indicate a footnote or special meaning, often appearing like a small star.
    - Example: Please see the **asterisk** at the bottom of the page for further details about the footnote.

4. **Disaster**: A sudden and widespread catastrophe, often metaphorically referred to as a "falling star."
    - Example: The earthquake was a **disaster** that affected thousands of people, leaving widespread devastation in its wake.

Word Duel: Astronomy vs. Disaster
Question: Which term relates to the study of stars and celestial objects?
  A.) Astronomy
  B.) Disaster
Correct Answer: Astronomy
Explanation: **Astronomy** is the scientific study of the stars and celestial bodies, while **disaster** refers to a catastrophic event, originally tied to the idea of "ill-fated stars" in ancient belief systems. **Astronomy** involves knowledge of the cosmos, while **disaster** refers to unfortunate events.

Semantic Scale: Stars and Their Influence
This scale shows different ways stars and celestial bodies can be perceived, from awe-inspiring phenomena to ominous events:

1. **Asterisk** – A small symbol resembling a star, often used to indicate a footnote or additional information.
    - Example: The **asterisk** on the form indicated there were more instructions at the bottom.
2. **Asteroid** – A rock or small planet that orbits the sun, often linked with space exploration.
    - Example: Scientists track the paths of **asteroids** to predict potential collisions with Earth.
3. **Astronomy** – The study of stars, planets, and celestial bodies.
    - Example: **Astronomy** enthusiasts often gather at observatories to watch meteor showers.

4. **Disaster** – A catastrophic event, sometimes linked to ancient beliefs in the ill omens of stars.
    - Example: The tsunami was a **disaster** that struck unexpectedly, causing massive destruction.

Language Time Travel: The Origin of "Aster-"

The prefix **"aster-"** comes from the Greek *astron*, which simply means "star." Ancient civilizations often used the stars for navigation and storytelling, attributing significant meaning to celestial events. Over time, **"aster-"** expanded beyond the literal stars to symbolize things that are important, noticeable, or prominent. The word **disaster**, for example, originally referred to an "ill star" or bad omen, suggesting that a bad event might be the result of a negative celestial influence. As science advanced, **"aster-"** became a core term in fields like astronomy, reflecting our ongoing fascination with the stars and the universe.

Story: The Stargazers' Discovery

In a small village by the sea, the local astronomer, Dr. Aster, was passionate about studying the stars. Every night, he would use his telescope to observe the night sky, cataloging planets, stars, and **asteroids**. One evening, as he watched the stars twinkle, he noticed something strange—a faint light that seemed to move across the sky. Could it be an undiscovered **asteroid**?

Excited, Dr. Aster rushed to the local observatory to share his findings. The discovery of the **asteroid** made headlines, drawing attention to the village and sparking an interest in **astronomy** among the locals. However, the excitement was short-lived when an unexpected event, a **disaster** in a nearby town, occurred. A terrible earthquake shook the region, and many believed it was a sign of the stars' warning.

Despite the tragedy, Dr. Aster remained optimistic, reminding everyone that just as the stars guide sailors,

astronomy can help us navigate the mysteries of the universe, offering both wonder and a deeper understanding of our place in the cosmos.

ROOT: "ANIM-" (MEANING: "LIFE" OR "SPIRIT")

The root **"anim-"** comes from the Latin *anima*, meaning "breath," "soul," or "life." This root appears in words that deal with life, spirit, or energy, emphasizing the essence of living things. It also often appears in terms related to motion or vitality.

Vocabulary:
1. **Animate**: To bring to life, or give motion to something that is not alive.
    - Example: The director's goal was to **animate** the characters with lifelike expressions and movements.
2. **Animal**: A living organism, typically one that is not a plant or a human, that moves and has sensory perception.
    - Example: The zoo houses a variety of **animals**, including lions, tigers, and bears.
3. **Animation**: The process of creating moving images from still pictures or drawings, often used in film and cartoons.
    - Example: **Animation** allows storytellers to bring their characters and worlds to life on the screen.
4. **Animosity**: Strong hostility or hatred, often used to

describe a deep-seated ill will or dislike.
- Example: The long-standing **animosity** between the two families made it difficult for them to cooperate on the project.

Word Duel: Animate vs. Animosity
Question: Which word refers to positive life or motion, and which to negative feelings of hostility?
    A.) Animate
    B.) Animosity

Correct Answer:
- **Animate**: **Animate** comes from the Latin *animare* (to give life), emphasizing vitality and motion.
- **Animosity**: Comes from the Latin *animositas*, which refers to a feeling of strong hostility, often associated with inner spirit or emotional energy, but in a negative sense.

Life vs. Hostility
This list compares the positive energy of life with the negative energy of conflict:

1. **Animate** – To bring to life, to give vitality and movement.
   - Example: The artist worked tirelessly to **animate** the characters in her short film.
2. **Animal** – A living creature, often one that is not human, with its own instincts and behaviors.
   - Example: The **animals** in the wild can be unpredictable and fierce.
3. **Animation** – The art or process of creating motion, typically used in movies or television.
   - Example: **Animation** allows for incredible creativity, as characters can defy the laws of physics.
4. **Animosity** – Strong, often bitter hostility or hatred.
   - Example: The old rivalry between the two companies led to much **animosity** in the

business world.

Language Time Travel: The Origin of "Anim-"
The root **"anim-"** comes from the Latin *anima*, meaning "soul," "spirit," or "breath." In ancient times, breath was considered the essence of life. The belief that life itself was imbued with a spirit or soul influenced the use of **"anim-"** in words that describe life and motion. Over time, the root evolved to also signify emotional energy, as seen in words like **animosity**. What started as a simple reference to the soul or spirit eventually expanded to encompass both living vitality and emotional forces.

Story: The Spirit of the Forest
In a secluded village nestled at the edge of a dense forest, people believed that the forest had a life of its own, a spirit that animated the trees and animals. The villagers called it **animus**, the life force that seemed to give motion to everything around them. The animals were believed to be its messengers, each one carrying the essence of the forest's **spirit**.

One day, a traveler arrived, skeptical of the villagers' beliefs. He thought of the forest as just trees and animals, nothing more. But as he wandered deeper into the woods, he felt an odd sense of peace and connection to the land. He observed the animals moving with purpose, and he saw the trees sway, as though they were alive with energy. His heart softened, and for the first time, he understood the **animation** of the forest—its **spirit** was real.

However, not everyone in the village shared his view. A local farmer, embittered by past losses, harbored **animosity** toward the forest. He blamed the trees for the hardships he had faced. He planned to cut them down, not understanding the sacred balance between life and nature. The traveler, now seeing the life force of the forest, tried to explain the importance of respect and balance, but the farmer's hatred blinded him to the truth. The forest, with its powerful **animosity** against destruction, fought back, creating a storm that protected its ancient trees.

The traveler left the village with a deep respect for the **spirit** of the forest, carrying with him the lesson that all life, from the smallest **animal** to the tallest tree, has its own **animus**, a force that should never be underestimated.

ROOT: "TACT-" (MEANING: "TOUCH")

The root **"tact-"** originates from the Latin *tangere*, which means "to touch" or "to handle." This root is used in words related to the sense of touch, contact, or the act of handling or managing situations with sensitivity.

Vocabulary:
1. **Tactile**: Relating to or involving the sense of touch.
    - Example: The blind man used a **tactile** map to navigate his way through the park.
2. **Contact**: The act of touching or communicating with someone or something.
    - Example: Please keep **contact** with the customer service team if you encounter any issues.
3. **Intact**: Remaining whole or undamaged, as if untouched.
    - Example: Despite the storm, the building remained **intact** and unharmed.
4. **Tactics**: Methods or strategies used to achieve a goal, often involving careful handling of situations.
    - Example: The general employed clever **tactics** to outsmart the enemy during the battle.

Word Duel: Tactile vs. Tactics

Question: Which word refers to physical touch, and which to strategic action?
- A.) Tactile
- B.) Tactics

Correct Answer:
- **Tactile** is directly related to touch, as in **tactile** sensations or textures, while Tactics refers to methods and strategies used to achieve an objective or goal.

Semantic Scale: Touch vs. Strategy

On this scale, **tact-** is used in both physical and strategic contexts:

1. **Tactile** – Pertaining to the sense of touch or physical interaction.
    - Example: The **tactile** experience of the soft fabric brought comfort to her.
2. **Contact** – The act of touching or establishing communication.
    - Example: After weeks of isolation, he finally made **contact** with his old friend.
3. **Intact** – Remaining undisturbed, unbroken, or untouched.
    - Example: The priceless artifact was found **intact** after the earthquake.
4. **Tactics** – The strategic use of action, often involving careful planning or handling of situations.
    - Example: He adjusted his **tactics** to win the chess match in the final moments.

Language Time Travel: The Origin of "Tact-"

The root **"tact-"** comes from the Latin word *tangere*, meaning "to touch." The concept of "touch" was central in ancient times, as it was both a physical and metaphorical way to convey connection, influence, or action. Over time, **"tact-"** evolved to include both the physical sensation of touch and the more abstract notions of handling or dealing with situations effectively, as in **tactics**.

Story: The Art of Tact

In a small coastal village, there was an old man named Luca who was known for his remarkable **tact** in handling even the most difficult situations. He had a special gift of connecting with people, making them feel heard and understood, all while maintaining peace in the community.

One day, a fierce debate arose over the use of the beach for tourists. The locals wanted to preserve the natural beauty of the area, while the tourists wanted better access and facilities. The argument became heated, and tensions were rising. The village council called upon Luca to help mediate the situation.

When Luca arrived at the council meeting, he sat quietly, observing the emotions of both sides. His approach was one of **tact**—listening to each side carefully, acknowledging their concerns, and then gently guiding them toward a compromise. He suggested building small access points for the tourists while preserving the most pristine areas. His idea was a perfect blend of practicality and respect for both sides, and the council was impressed by his **tactics** of diplomacy.

Thanks to Luca's clever handling, the dispute was resolved without animosity. The village remained **intact**—both the peacefulness of the community and the beauty of the beach were preserved. His skillful use of **tact** and **tactics** made him a beloved figure in the village, and his legacy lived on as a model for future generations on how to handle even the most delicate issues with grace and wisdom.

ROOT: "BIBL-" (MEANING: "BOOK")

The root **"bibl-"** comes from the Greek word *biblion*, meaning "book" or "scroll." It's often associated with anything related to books, reading, and literature, reflecting the importance of written works in human history and knowledge transmission.

Vocabulary:
1. **Bibliography**: A list of books or written works, typically used in research or academic contexts.
    - Example: The student's **bibliography** included a wide range of scholarly sources for the research paper.
2. **Bible**: A sacred or authoritative text, most notably the Christian Bible.
    - Example: Many scholars have dedicated their lives to studying the **Bible** and its historical context.
3. **Bibliophile**: A person who loves or collects books, especially rare or valuable ones.
    - Example: As a **bibliophile**, she spent hours browsing through antique bookstores, searching for unique editions.
4. **Bibliomania**: An obsession with collecting books, often to the point of excess.
    - Example: His **bibliomania** led him to

accumulate thousands of books, filling every corner of his house.

Word Duel: Bibliophile vs. Bibliomania

Question: Which term refers to a person who loves books, and which refers to an obsession with collecting them?

    A.) Bibliophile
    B.) Bibliomania

Correct Answer:

- **Bibliophile** is a lover of books, someone who enjoys reading and collecting them as a passion, while Bibliomania is an excessive or uncontrollable desire to collect books, often leading to an overwhelming accumulation.

Love for Books vs. Obsession

1. **Bibliophile** – A person who appreciates and collects books in moderation.
   - Example: The **bibliophile** carefully curated her collection of rare first editions.
2. **Bibliomania** – An intense obsession with books, often to the point of hoarding.
   - Example: His **bibliomania** led him to buy hundreds of books at auction, even though he had no space left on his shelves.

Language Time Travel: The Origin of "Bibl-"

The term **"bibl-"** comes from the Greek word *biblion*, meaning "book." The ancient city of Byblos, a significant trading hub in antiquity, was famous for its export of papyrus, a material used for writing. As such, the word *biblion* became associated with books, and eventually, all things written or related to written works. Over time, it evolved into words like **bibliography** (a list of books) and **bibliophile** (a lover of books).

Story: The Legacy of Books

In a small town, there was a humble library that housed a vast collection of books. It wasn't large, but it had something special—it was filled with rare volumes that only a few people had ever heard of. Among those who loved the library was an elderly man named Mr. Thomas, a **bibliophile** who treasured books more than anything else in the world.

One day, a fire broke out near the town's square, and the flames threatened to consume the library. As the fire spread, Mr. Thomas rushed to the library, determined to save his beloved collection. The townspeople tried to stop him, but his love for the books was so great that he ignored their pleas. He managed to save a few precious tomes, but the rest of the collection was lost to the flames.

After the fire, the people of the town decided to rebuild the library. This time, they added a **bibliography** of the library's collection as a tribute to the books they had lost. Mr. Thomas, though heartbroken, knew that the legacy of the books would live on. As the new library rose from the ashes, he realized that his **bibliomania** had given the town a deeper appreciation for the value of books, and he took solace in the knowledge that the love for reading would never die.

ROOT: "PLAC-" (MEANING: "PLEASE" OR "CALM")

The root **"plac-"** comes from the Latin word *placare*, which means "to please" or "to calm." Words derived from this root often describe actions that soothe, calm, or make things more agreeable.

Vocabulary:
1. **Placate**: To make someone less angry or hostile by pleasing or calming them.
    - Example: The manager tried to **placate** the upset customer by offering a refund.
2. **Implacable**: Unable to be calmed or appeased; relentless or unforgiving.
    - Example: Despite all attempts to reason with him, his anger remained **implacable**.
3. **Placidity**: The quality of being calm and peaceful.
    - Example: The **placidity** of the lake at dawn was a perfect backdrop for meditation.
4. **Placid**: Calm and peaceful, with little movement or disturbance.
    - Example: The **placid** waters of the river made it an ideal spot for a relaxing boat ride.

Word Duel: Placate vs. Implacable
Question: Which word describes the act of calming someone, and which refers to someone who cannot be calmed?

A.) Placate
B.) Implacable

Correct Answer:
- **Placate** is the act of making someone less upset or angry, often through soothing actions or words, while Implacable describes a person or thing that cannot be calmed or satisfied, often remaining in a state of anger or conflict.

Semantic Scale: Levels of Calmness
This scale illustrates the progression from a minor sense of calm to an extreme, unshakable calm:

1. **Placid** – Calm and peaceful in appearance, not easily disturbed.

Example: The **placid** lake mirrored the clear sky above.

2. **Placidity** – The state or quality of being calm and peaceful.

Example: The **placidity** of the countryside provided a perfect escape from the hustle and bustle of city life.

3. **Placate** – To soothe or calm someone, often after they have been upset.

Example: She tried to **placate** her angry friend by offering a sincere apology.

4. **Implacable** – A state of being unable to be calmed, showing no signs of yielding.

Example: The **implacable** enemy forces showed no mercy, even after repeated attempts to negotiate peace.

Language Time Travel: The Origin of "Plac-"
The root **"plac-"** comes from the Latin *placare*, meaning "to please or calm." Ancient Romans used the word to refer to actions or gestures that were intended to soothe or make others happy, such as gifts, conciliatory gestures, or kind words. Over time, the root found its way into various words in English, each relating to the concept of soothing, pleasing, or calming others.

Story: The Peaceful Town

In a small, serene village nestled by the hills, the people were known for their **placid** nature. The gentle flow of the river and the lush green forests around them created a sense of **placidity** that touched every part of their lives. However, one summer, a disagreement arose between the villagers and the neighboring town over the rights to the river.

The mayor of the village, known for his calm demeanor, tried his best to **placate** the angry townspeople from the neighboring area. He spoke kindly, offering compromises and peaceful solutions, but the anger from the other side only grew. Their leader, an **implacable** man, refused to negotiate, his wrath unwavering no matter the peaceful gestures made.

Despite his best efforts, the mayor could not calm the fury of the neighboring leader. But the villagers, undeterred by the **implacable** opposition, continued their peaceful existence. In the end, the wisdom of calm prevailed, as the dispute settled through time, and the village's quiet, **placid** beauty remained.

The lesson was clear: while one can always try to **placate** others, some situations remain beyond reason. Yet, peace and **placidity** were more powerful than any anger, for they sustained the village in a way that no conflict could ever disturb.

ROOT: "POL-" (MEANING: "CITY" OR "COMMUNITY")

The root **"pol-"** comes from the Greek word *polis*, which means "city" or "community." This root is widely used in words that relate to urban life, government, and societal structures. It reflects the idea of a group of people living together in a community or a city, often with organized systems, laws, and structures.

Vocabulary:
1. **Metropolis**: A large and significant city, often a central hub of culture, economy, and politics.
    - Example: New York City is a global **metropolis**, bustling with culture, finance, and people from around the world.
2. **Politics**: The activities, actions, and policies used to gain and hold power in a government or to influence the government.
    - Example: The debates during the election were filled with **political** arguments about healthcare and education.
3. **Cosmopolitan**: A person who is at ease in many different countries or cultures; or something that contains a wide variety of cultures or people.

- Example: London is known for being a **cosmopolitan** city, where you can find a blend of cultures and languages from around the world.
4. **Police**: The organized body of people responsible for maintaining public order, enforcing laws, and preventing crime in a city or community.
    - Example: The **police** were called to handle the protest that had escalated in the city square.

Word Duel: Politics vs. Police
Question: Which word refers to the actions related to government and power, and which word refers to the law enforcement in a city or community?
  A.) Politics
  B.) Police

Correct Answer:
- **Politics** is the conduct of government, decision-making, and power distribution within a community or nation, while Police is the individuals and organization tasked with maintaining law and order within a city or town.

City & Society
This list illustrates various terms connected to cities and communities, from broad concepts to more specific aspects:
1. **Cosmopolitan** – A person or place that is familiar with and welcoming to people from many cultures and countries.

Example: The **cosmopolitan** atmosphere of the international festival made it a unique event.

2. **Metropolis** – A large and important city, typically a hub for economic, cultural, and political activity.

Example: Tokyo is a **metropolis**, where both ancient traditions and cutting-edge technology coexist.

3. **Politics** – The activities, debates, and processes associated with governance and the distribution of

power in a society.
Example: The **political** landscape in the country is changing rapidly as new leaders emerge.

4. **Police** – The authorities responsible for enforcing laws and keeping order within the city or community.

Example: The **police** patrolled the streets to ensure the safety of all citizens during the event.

Language Time Travel: The Origin of "Pol-"

The root **"pol-"** comes from the Greek word *polis*, which referred to a city or a community with a governing system. The concept of the **polis** was central in Ancient Greece, where the **polis** was more than just a city—it was a fully developed society with its own politics, laws, and civic life. Over time, the meaning of the root expanded into various aspects of city life, governance, and social organization.

Story: The Rise of the Polis

Long ago in ancient Greece, there was a small village nestled at the base of a hill. The people there lived simple lives, working the land and living in harmony with nature. But as their community grew, they realized that living together required more than just agriculture—it required organization, laws, and systems of governance.

As the village grew into a **polis**, the people established a council to make decisions and solve disputes. They began to develop a sense of community that extended beyond mere survival; they created a place where **politics** became a way of organizing and making decisions that affected everyone in the **polis**.

In this new city, life wasn't just about farming or commerce; it was about living together with shared values, managing resources, and maintaining order. Eventually, the **polis** expanded into a large **metropolis**, a city bustling with trade, culture, and ideas.

With this expansion, new challenges arose. The city needed a force to keep order, protect the citizens, and ensure that the laws of the **polis** were upheld. Thus, the **police** were established, a group of men and women tasked with maintaining peace and enforcing the laws of the city.

As centuries passed, the influence of the **polis** grew, and its legacy continued to shape cities around the world. Whether in the form of **metropolises** or the **police** keeping order, the concept of living together in organized communities remained central to human civilization.

And so, the city, once just a small community, evolved into a thriving center of civilization, governed by **politics** and watched over by the **police**.

ROOT: "FLOR-" (MEANING: "FLOWER")

The root **"flor-"** comes from the Latin word *flora*, which refers to the goddess of flowers in Roman mythology, and by extension, to the flowers themselves. It symbolizes the natural beauty, growth, and life found in the plant kingdom. This root appears in words related to flowers, plants, and anything associated with blooming or flourishing life.

Vocabulary:
1. **Flora**: Refers to the plants of a particular region or period, or can be used to describe the collective plant life of a place.
    - Example: The **flora** of the rainforest is incredibly diverse, with thousands of species of plants and trees.
2. **Floral**: Relating to flowers; often used to describe patterns, designs, or decorations that feature flowers.
    - Example: She wore a beautiful **floral** dress with roses and daisies on it.
3. **Florist**: A person or business that sells flowers and plants.
    - Example: The **florist** created a stunning bouquet of lilies and roses for the wedding.
4. **Defloration**: The act of removing flowers from a plant or, in historical contexts, an old term referring

to the loss of virginity.
- Example: In botany, **defloration** can refer to the removal or cutting of flowers from a plant.

Word Duel: Floral vs. Flora
Question: What's the difference between **flora** and **floral**?
- **Flora** refers to the collective plants or flowers in a particular area or environment.
- **Floral** describes anything related to flowers, such as patterns, decorations, or designs featuring flowers.

Semantic Scale: From Flower to Life
This scale connects terms related to flowers and plant life, emphasizing different aspects of the plant kingdom:
1. **Flora** – The collective plants or flowers of a region, often used in scientific or ecological contexts.

Example: The **flora** of the desert is adapted to survive with minimal water.

2. **Floral** – Describes things that are related to flowers, such as designs or scents.

Example: The **floral** fragrance of the garden filled the air on a warm spring day.

3. **Florist** – A person who sells or arranges flowers.

Example: The **florist** delivered a beautiful bouquet to my house for my birthday.

4. **Defloration** – Historically used to describe the act of removing flowers from a plant or, metaphorically, the loss of virginity.

Example: The **defloration** of the plant was done to collect its flowers for the garden.

Language Time Travel: The Origin of "Flor-"
The root **"flor-"** comes from the Latin word *flora*, which is both the name of the Roman goddess of flowers and the term for plant life in general. The goddess Flora was revered as a symbol of spring and the renewal of life through flowers, making her a central figure in the annual celebrations of blooming and

growth. As the centuries passed, the use of *flora* evolved to refer to the collective plant life of any region, while words like **floral** emerged to describe things related to flowers.

Story: The Birth of Flora

In ancient Rome, **Flora** was a beloved goddess, the personification of the blossoming flowers and the vibrant renewal of nature in spring. Her influence was felt across the land, as people celebrated the arrival of new life each year with festivals and offerings to honor her. As the Romans celebrated the beauty and bounty of the blooming flowers, they also began to use her name to refer to the rich variety of plants in their world. The word *flora* began to represent the plants that grew in any region, and the symbolism of flowers as a sign of life, beauty, and growth spread across cultures.

As time passed, **flora** became the term used by botanists and naturalists to describe the collection of plants in a particular area. Meanwhile, **floral** became synonymous with anything adorned by flowers, whether in decoration, design, or scent. The roots of **flor-** continued to flourish through history, and the work of **florists** kept the tradition of flowers alive, ensuring that each bouquet carried not only the beauty of nature but also the legacy of Flora herself.

ROOT: "LITH-" (MEANING: "STONE" OR "ROCK")

The root **"lith-"** comes from the Greek word *lithos*, meaning "stone" or "rock." This root is used to form words that are related to stones, rocks, or the materials associated with them. Throughout history, the concept of stones and rocks has symbolized permanence, durability, and the foundations of nature and civilization.

Vocabulary:
1. **Lithograph**: A method of printing that involves drawing on a flat stone or metal plate, typically used for artistic prints.
    - Example: The artist created a **lithograph** of the cityscape, capturing the intricate details of the skyline.
2. **Monolith**: A large, upright stone, often used in ancient architecture or monuments.
    - Example: The **monolith** stood tall in the middle of the desert, a mysterious and solitary landmark.
3. **Paleolithic**: Referring to the early phase of the Stone Age, characterized by the use of primitive stone tools.
    - Example: The **Paleolithic** era is known for the development of simple tools and early human settlements.

4. **Neolithic**: Relating to the later part of the Stone Age, when agriculture and permanent settlements began.
    - Example: The **Neolithic** period marked the transition from hunting and gathering to farming.

Word Duel: Monolith vs. Lithograph

Question: What's the difference between **monolith** and **lithograph**?

- A **monolith** is a large, upright stone, often a single block or rock that stands as a monument or landmark.
- A **lithograph** is a type of print made from a drawing or design on a stone or metal plate, typically used in art and publishing.

From Stone to Art

This list connects terms related to stones, rocks, and how they are represented or used in different contexts:

1. **Monolith** – A large, singular stone, often used in monumental structures or as a symbol of permanence.
    - Example: The ancient **monolith** is a relic of a civilization that revered the power of rock and stone.
2. **Lithograph** – A print created by drawing on a flat stone or metal plate, used in art and printmaking.
    - Example: The artist's **lithograph** of the mountain landscape captured its rugged beauty.
3. **Paleolithic** – The prehistoric era marked by the use of stone tools, hunting, and gathering.
    - Example: Early humans lived during the **Paleolithic** period, relying on rudimentary tools made from stone.
4. **Neolithic** – The later phase of the Stone Age, marked by agricultural development and the advent of permanent settlements.
    - Example: The **Neolithic** Revolution changed

human history by introducing farming and building communities.

Language Time Travel: The Origin of "Lith-"

The root **"lith-"** is derived from the Greek word *lithos*, meaning "stone" or "rock." In ancient Greece, the word was used to refer to both physical stones and symbolic concepts of enduring strength and permanence. This root was adopted into various European languages, particularly in terms like **monolith** (a large stone) and **lithograph** (a print made from stone). Over time, **lith-** evolved into terms that have been integral to our understanding of early human history, such as **Paleolithic** (early Stone Age) and **Neolithic** (later Stone Age), highlighting the importance of stones in the development of civilization.

Story: The Legacy of Lithos

In ancient Greek mythology, **Lithos** was often associated with both the physical and symbolic power of stones. Stones were revered for their durability and endurance, qualities that humans aspired to embody. As early humans began to carve and shape stones for tools and monuments, they recognized the profound impact these "stones" had on their survival and growth.

The word **lithos** became synonymous with both the tools that helped shape early human society and the monuments that lasted through the ages. The **monoliths** of ancient cultures, towering stones that stood as markers of time and power, became symbols of human achievement, representing an unyielding strength that could withstand the test of time. As civilizations grew, the art of **lithography** was born, capturing the precision and artistry of stone through prints that could be replicated.

In the world of prehistoric humans, the **Paleolithic** era was defined by the use of basic stone tools, shaping early life. Later, as agriculture and society advanced, the **Neolithic** period was born, a time when humans transitioned from simple stone tools to more complex innovations.

The legacy of **lithos**, the stone, continued to define both the natural world and the artistic world, reminding humanity of its connection to the earth, to permanence, and to the enduring power of stone.

ROOT: "CHROM-" (MEANING: "COLOR")

The root **"chrom-"** originates from the Greek word *khrōma*, meaning "color." This root is often used to describe various aspects of color, including the variation of hues, shades, or the presence of color in different contexts. Over time, this root has been extended to scientific and artistic terminology, denoting anything related to color, as well as its interaction with light and matter.

Vocabulary:
1. **Chromatic**: Relating to or produced by color, often used in the context of color scales or harmonies.
    - Example: The artist's **chromatic** palette included vibrant reds and blues, creating a striking contrast in the painting.
2. **Monochrome**: Consisting of one color or shades of one color, often used in photography or design.
    - Example: The **monochrome** photograph captured the essence of the scene in varying shades of black and white.
3. **Chromosome**: A threadlike structure made of protein and nucleic acids that carries genetic information, derived from the fact that chromosomes stain vividly with certain dyes.

- Example: Human cells contain 23 pairs of **chromosomes**, which carry the genetic instructions for development.
4. **Polychrome**: Featuring many colors; often used to describe multi-colored art or decoration.
    - Example: The **polychrome** sculpture was intricately painted, with bright and bold colors that brought it to life.

Word Duel: Monochrome vs. Polychrome
Question: What's the difference between **monochrome** and **polychrome**?
- **Monochrome** refers to something made using only one color or variations of a single color, such as black-and-white photography.
- **Polychrome** refers to something that uses many colors, often in a rich or decorative way, such as a multi-colored painting or sculpture.

Semantic Scale: From Single Color to Many
This scale shows the evolution of terms from simple, singular colors to more complex mixtures:
1. **Monochrome** – A design or piece of art created using one color or its shades.
    - Example: The **monochrome** design gives the room a minimalist, serene feel.
2. **Chromatic** – Pertaining to color, or having a range of colors.
    - Example: The **chromatic** scale used in the music reflected the emotional depth of the performance.
3. **Polychrome** – Multicolored, often referring to artwork or decoration.
    - Example: The church's **polychrome** stained-glass windows depicted vibrant biblical scenes.

Language Time Travel: The Origin of "Chrom-"
The root **"chrom-"** comes from the Greek word *khrōma*, which

means "color." In ancient Greek, *khrōma* was used to describe the idea of color in nature, art, and design. Over time, the root spread to other languages and took on specific meanings in science, art, and biology. It was particularly influential in fields like chemistry and genetics, where it was used to describe the colorful properties of certain substances, such as the staining properties of **chromosomes**. The development of **chromatic** scales in art and music further solidified its importance in understanding the concept of color.

Story: The Evolution of Color in Language

Color has always played an essential role in human perception, creativity, and communication. In ancient Greece, **khrōma** was more than just a word for a physical property; it was tied to the fundamental experience of the world around them. From early depictions of natural scenes in **monochrome** paintings to the rich, multi-colored designs in Greek pottery, the use of color evolved.

As humans developed their understanding of the natural world, they saw that color could not only define aesthetics but also biology. The term **chromosome**, coined in the 19th century, reflected this new understanding, as scientists discovered that chromosomes were vividly stained with color during cell division, giving a visual representation of genetic inheritance.

Meanwhile, artists and designers embraced the beauty of color, giving rise to the concept of **polychrome** art, which used multiple colors to create vivid, dynamic works. Whether in painting, sculpture, or even music (with **chromatic** scales), color became an important tool for both expression and understanding in human culture.

ROOT: "ECO-" (MEANING: "HOUSE" OR "ENVIRONMENT")

The root **"eco-"** comes from the Greek word *oikos*, meaning "house" or "household." Over time, the meaning expanded to encompass the broader concept of the environment and all systems within it. In modern usage, **eco-** is widely associated with ecological and environmental contexts, including the study of organisms, their interactions with the environment, and the balance of natural systems. Additionally, it can refer to the management and organization of resources, such as in **economy**, which originally focused on household management before evolving to mean the broader system of resource distribution and wealth.

Vocabulary:
1. **Ecology**: The study of organisms and their interactions with each other and their environment.
    - Example: The **ecology** of a rainforest is complex, with many species depending on each other for survival.
2. **Ecosystem**: A community of living organisms and their interactions with their physical environment.
    - Example: Coral reefs are a vital **ecosystem**, providing habitat for a wide variety of

marine life.
3. **Economy**: The system of production, distribution, and consumption of goods and services in a society, originating from the management of household resources.
    - Example: The global **economy** has been impacted by various factors, including trade policies and technological advancements.
4. **Ecological**: Pertaining to the relationship between living organisms and their environment.
    - Example: The **ecological** consequences of deforestation can be devastating, leading to loss of biodiversity and climate change.

Word Duel: Ecology vs. Economy

Question: What's the connection between **ecology** and **economy**?

- **Ecology** refers to the study of the environment and living organisms' relationships with it, focusing on nature's balance.
- **Economy** involves the management of resources, wealth, and production in society, but originally had its roots in managing the "household" environment.

While the two fields are distinct, they intersect when considering sustainable practices and environmental conservation, where economic decisions are made with ecological impacts in mind.

From Household to Global Systems

This list shows how **eco-** has evolved from a concept related to individual homes to global systems:

1. **Economy** – Originally referring to the management of household resources, it now encompasses the global system of production and consumption.

Example: The rise of **economy** in global trade networks reshaped societies and cultures across the world.

2. **Ecology** – The scientific study of ecosystems and

environmental interactions.

Example: The study of **ecology** helps us understand the delicate balance of nature and the importance of preserving ecosystems.

3. **Ecosystem** – A community of organisms interacting with each other and their physical environment.

Example: Each species in an **ecosystem** has a role, contributing to the overall health of the system.

Language Time Travel: The Origin of "Eco-"

The root **"eco-"** originates from the Greek word *oikos*, meaning "house" or "household." In ancient Greek, it referred to the management of a household, and over time, the term expanded to include the concept of managing and maintaining the balance of the environment. During the 19th century, with the development of ecological science, **eco-** became associated with the study of nature and ecosystems, as scientists began to understand the importance of the interdependence of organisms within their environment. Today, **eco-** is used widely in environmental, economic, and scientific contexts, symbolizing the importance of balance, sustainability, and the interconnectedness of all systems.

Story: The Evolution of "Eco-"

From its humble beginnings in ancient Greece, where *oikos* referred to the management of a household, the **"eco-"** root has grown to symbolize a much broader, interconnected concept. The word **economy** once described how resources within a household were managed, but now it represents the global system of production, distribution, and consumption. In contrast, **ecology**, which emerged in the 19th century, focuses on the relationships between organisms and their environment.

As our understanding of the natural world deepened, so did the relevance of **eco-** in describing the balance of nature. Ecologists have long studied the interdependent relationships between organisms and their surroundings, and today, the idea of sustainability influences economic policies and environmental practices worldwide. Whether in **ecosystems**, which describe complex networks of life, or in the global **economy**, which considers resource management on a macro scale, **eco-** remains a critical concept for understanding and preserving our world.

ROOT: "ORTH-" (MEANING: "STRAIGHT" OR "CORRECT")

The root **"orth-"** comes from the Greek word *orthos*, meaning "straight," "correct," or "upright." Over time, this root has expanded in its usage to indicate correctness, proper alignment, or conformity to a set standard. In medical terms, **orth-** is commonly used to refer to the correction of physical issues such as those with bones or teeth, while in general usage, it can refer to adherence to established principles or beliefs.

Vocabulary:
1. **Orthopedic**: Relating to the correction of deformities or disorders of the bones and muscles.
    - Example: The **orthopedic** surgeon specialized in fixing fractures and correcting joint issues.
2. **Orthodontist**: A dental specialist who corrects teeth and jaw alignment.
    - Example: After years of braces, the **orthodontist** helped straighten my teeth into a perfect smile.
3. **Orthodox**: Adhering to traditional or established beliefs, practices, or doctrines.

- Example: The community followed **orthodox** teachings, maintaining the long-standing customs of their faith.
  4. **Orthography**: The conventional spelling system of a language.
     - Example: The study of **orthography** is crucial for understanding how different languages develop their writing systems.

Brief Story: The Origin of "Orth-"

The root **"orth-"** originates from the Greek *orthos*, meaning "straight," "right," or "correct." In ancient Greek, the concept of *orthos* was closely tied to ideas of balance, truth, and the proper way to do things. Over time, this sense of "rightness" extended beyond physical alignment to broader ideas of correctness in beliefs, practices, and structures. For example, in medicine, **orthopedic** practices emerged to address the correction of physical misalignments, such as broken bones or skeletal deformities. Similarly, **orthodontics** focused on straightening teeth. The use of **orth-** in words like **orthodox** emphasizes correctness according to tradition or established norms, while **orthography** refers to the standardization of written language.

Language Timeline: "Orth-" Across Disciplines

- **Orthopedic**: Medical term for correcting musculoskeletal issues. Example: The **orthopedic** doctor advised surgery to correct the misaligned hip.
- **Orthodontist**: Dental specialist focusing on teeth alignment. Example: **Orthodontist** care helped improve my bite and smile.
- **Orthodox**: A term for adhering to traditional principles or doctrines. Example: His **orthodox** views on education were rooted in classical methods.
- **Orthography**: Refers to the rules of spelling and writing in a language. Example: Correcting errors in **orthography** is essential when learning a new language.

ROOT: "CARN-" (MEANING: "FLESH" OR "MEAT")

The root **"carn-"** comes from the Latin word *caro, carnis*, meaning "flesh" or "meat." It is often associated with terms that involve living creatures, particularly in relation to their bodies or consumption of flesh. The root has also taken on broader symbolic meanings, such as in the case of **incarnation**, which refers to a being or spirit taking on a physical body.

Vocabulary:
1. **Carnivore**: An animal that feeds primarily on meat.
    - Example: The **carnivore** stalked its prey through the forest, using its sharp teeth to tear through the flesh.
2. **Incarnation**: The embodiment of a deity or spirit in a physical form; in Christianity, it specifically refers to the belief in the embodiment of God in the person of Jesus Christ.
    - Example: In Christian doctrine, the **incarnation** is the moment when the divine became flesh in the person of Jesus.
3. **Carnage**: The killing of a large number of people or animals, often in a violent or bloody manner.
    - Example: The battlefield was strewn with the aftermath of **carnage**, with bodies lying everywhere.

4. **Reincarnate**: To be reborn into a new body after death, in the belief system of reincarnation.
    - Example: In some cultures, it is believed that after death, a soul will **reincarnate** into a new form.

The Origin of "Carn-"

The root **"carn-"** has its origins in Latin, specifically from the word *caro* or *carnis*, which meant "flesh" or "meat." This root is linked to the physical body and the nourishment derived from flesh, typically in reference to animals or human bodies. Over time, the concept of **"flesh"** and **"meat"** expanded into various spiritual and philosophical ideas, such as **incarnation**, which refers to a divine being becoming physically embodied in the world. The root also connects to **carnage**, where large-scale death or slaughter is referenced, and **carnivore**, indicating an animal that consumes only flesh. The evolution of the root reflects both physical and metaphorical meanings tied to life, death, and the human body.

Language Timeline: "Carn-" Across Disciplines

- **Carnivore**: Refers to animals that rely on eating meat for survival. Example: Lions, tigers, and other **carnivores** are at the top of the food chain.
- **Incarnation**: In theology, it refers to a deity taking a physical form. Example: The **incarnation** of gods in mythology often symbolizes their interaction with the human world.
- **Carnage**: Describes large-scale violence or bloodshed. Example: The **carnage** of war often leaves deep scars on a society.
- **Reincarnate**: A concept in certain religions where the soul is reborn. Example: The belief in **reincarnation** is central to Hinduism and Buddhism.

ROOT: "PNEU-" (MEANING: "BREATH" OR "LUNG")

The root **"pneu-"** is derived from the Greek word *pneuma*, which means "breath," "spirit," or "wind." In modern medical terms, it is often associated with conditions and devices related to the lungs and respiratory system. The root reflects both the literal and metaphorical connections to air and breathing, vital components of life.

Vocabulary:
1. **Pneumonia**: An infection that inflames the air sacs of one or both lungs, often causing symptoms like coughing, fever, and difficulty breathing.
    - Example: The patient was diagnosed with **pneumonia** after a series of coughing fits and shortness of breath.
2. **Pneumatic**: Pertaining to or operated by air or gas under pressure; often used in reference to tools or systems that use compressed air.
    - Example: The factory used **pneumatic** drills to break through tough rock during construction.
3. **Apnea**: A condition characterized by temporary cessation of breathing, especially during sleep, as seen in sleep apnea.
    - Example: People with **sleep apnea** often

experience interruptions in their breathing patterns while asleep.
4. **Pneumonectomy**: A surgical procedure in which a lung is removed, often due to cancer or severe lung disease.
    - Example: The doctor recommended a **pneumonectomy** after the tumor in the patient's lung could not be removed by other means.

The Origin of "Pneu-"

The root **"pneu-"** originates from the Greek word *pneuma*, meaning "breath" or "wind." This term was initially used in ancient philosophy to describe the soul, seen as something akin to breath or air. Over time, it evolved into a medical term specifically linked to the lungs and respiratory processes. In the 19th and 20th centuries, as the field of medicine developed, terms such as **pneumonia** and **pneumonectomy** came to represent various conditions and procedures directly involving the lungs. The **"pneu-"** root now forms the basis for numerous medical terms concerning breathing and lung function, reflecting both the physical and essential role of air in sustaining life.

Language Timeline: "Pneu-" Across Disciplines
- **Pneumonia**: Refers to an infection of the lungs that affects the ability to breathe properly.
- **Pneumatic**: Describes systems, tools, or machines powered by compressed air or gases.
- **Apnea**: Often used in medical contexts to describe a temporary stoppage of breathing, particularly during sleep.
- **Pneumonectomy**: A surgical procedure involving the removal of a lung, often to treat cancer or other severe diseases of the lungs.

ROOT: "MATER-" (MEANING: "MOTHER")

The root "mater-" comes from the Latin word *mater*, meaning "mother." It symbolizes the concepts of origin, nurturing, and the supportive foundation found in family and society. This root is often used in words that relate to motherhood, caregiving, and central structures of care or authority. Words with "mater-" often evoke ideas of protection, sustenance, and guidance.

Vocabulary:
1. **Maternity**: Relating to motherhood, especially during pregnancy and childbirth.
   - *Example*: The hospital has a dedicated maternity ward to care for mothers and their newborns.
2. **Maternal**: Pertaining to a mother or motherly qualities, such as care and nurturing.
   - *Example*: Her maternal instincts kicked in as she comforted the crying child.
3. **Matriarch**: A woman who is the head or leader of a family or community.
   - *Example*: The matriarch of the family gathered everyone for an annual celebration.
4. **Matrix**: An environment or structure in which something develops; also used in biology and mathematics to refer to a supporting structure or

arrangement.
- *Example*: The family is often seen as the matrix in which children develop and grow.

Word Duel: Maternal vs. Maternity
Question: What's the difference between maternal and maternity?
- **Maternal** describes qualities or instincts related to a mother, such as being caring or nurturing.
- **Maternity** specifically refers to motherhood, especially in the context of pregnancy and childbirth.

Semantic Scale: From Motherhood to Authority
This scale connects terms related to motherhood, caregiving, and foundational structures, highlighting different aspects of maternal influence:

1. **Maternity** – Refers to motherhood or pregnancy, especially in medical or care contexts.

   Example: The maternity leave policy ensures that new mothers have time to care for their babies.

2. **Maternal** – Relates to qualities or behaviors associated with a mother.

   Example: She displayed maternal warmth when looking after her younger siblings.

3. **Matriarch** – A female leader, often the head of a family or community.

   Example: As the matriarch, she upheld family traditions and values.

4. **Matrix** – An origin or environment in which something develops; often used metaphorically.

   Example: The educational system acts as a matrix for intellectual growth.

Language Time Travel: The Origin of "Mater-"
The root "mater-" comes from the Latin word *mater*, which directly translates to "mother." In ancient societies, the role of the mother was seen as fundamental to family and community life, symbolizing care, growth, and guidance. Over

time, the maternal role became synonymous with nurturing environments and structures that support growth. The word *maternity* became associated specifically with pregnancy and birth, while *maternal* described motherly qualities. Meanwhile, *matriarch* and *matrix* extended the root's use to describe female authority and foundational environments, reflecting the protective and nurturing qualities of motherhood across various contexts.

Story: The Essence of Mater

In ancient Rome, the word *mater* was more than a title—it embodied the idea of nurturing life and sustaining the family. The mother was central to family structure, symbolizing both physical and emotional support. As society evolved, words derived from *mater* grew in meaning. *Maternity* came to represent the special period of pregnancy and childbirth, while *maternal* captured the essence of motherly care. The *matriarch*, as the head of a family, wielded wisdom and authority, passing traditions and values to future generations. Even the word *matrix* developed to symbolize an environment that nurtures and sustains growth, echoing the fundamental role of a mother in the world. Each word with *mater-* carries forward the legacy of care, protection, and life-giving strength associated with mothers throughout history.

ROOT: "UNI-" (MEANING: "ONE")

The root "uni-" comes from the Latin word *unus*, meaning "one." It represents concepts of singularity, unity, and oneness. Words derived from "uni-" often convey ideas of bringing together, forming a single entity, or having a uniform quality. This root appears in words that emphasize unity, alignment, or an undivided approach.

Vocabulary:
1. **Unify**: To bring together or combine into a single unit.
   - *Example*: The leader's goal was to unify the community around a common cause.
2. **Uniform**: Identical or consistent; also refers to a standard outfit worn by members of an organization.
   - *Example*: The team members wore a uniform to create a sense of unity and belonging.
3. **Unilateral**: Involving or decided by one side or party only.
   - *Example*: The company made a unilateral decision to change the policy without consulting the employees.
4. **Unity**: The state of being united or joined as a whole.
   - *Example*: The celebration fostered a sense of unity among people from different backgrounds.

Word Duel: Unify vs. Unity

Question: What's the difference between unify and unity?
- **Unify** is a verb that means to bring together or combine separate parts into a single entity.
- **Unity** is a noun that describes the state of being united or joined together as one.

From Oneness to Uniformity

This list connects terms related to the idea of oneness, highlighting different aspects of unity and singularity:
1. **Unify** – To bring together separate parts to form a single unit.
   - *Example*: Efforts were made to unify the team, creating stronger collaboration.
2. **Uniform** – Identical or consistent in appearance or character, often symbolizing unity.
   - *Example*: The employees wore a uniform to represent the organization.
3. **Unilateral** – Refers to actions or decisions made by one side only.
   - *Example*: The unilateral decision affected everyone but involved no consultation.
4. **Unity** – The quality or state of being one, often signifying harmony and togetherness.
   - *Example*: Unity in the group grew as they worked toward a shared goal.

Language Time Travel: The Origin of "Uni-"

The root "uni-" stems from the Latin word *unus*, meaning "one." In ancient Roman society, the concept of oneness was central to ideas of unity and harmony, whether in family, community, or governance. Over time, the root *uni-* evolved to represent not only the idea of singularity but also the value of combining parts into a cohesive whole. As language developed, words like *unify* and *unity* emerged, emphasizing the importance of togetherness, while *uniform* highlighted the visual consistency symbolizing unity. The term *unilateral* extended the root to describe actions or decisions involving a single party, often implying a singular direction. Together, these words preserve the notion of unity and oneness, underscoring the importance of harmony in both individual and collective contexts.

Story: The Power of Unity

In ancient Rome, the idea of *unus*, or "one," symbolized strength and cohesion. Communities valued unity, believing that harmony was key to enduring challenges. Over centuries, words derived from *uni-* developed to express this principle. Leaders who sought to *unify* people around a common vision became symbols of strength. The concept of *unity* took root as individuals joined together, finding strength in numbers. With the rise of organized groups, *uniforms* emerged to foster a sense of belonging, and *unilateral* decisions showcased the importance of a clear, singular direction. Words with *uni-* continue to remind us that unity, whether in appearance, action, or purpose, brings individuals together, highlighting the timeless strength found in oneness.

ROOT: "FER-" (MEANING: "CARRY" OR "BRING")

The root "fer-" comes from the Latin verb *ferre*, which means "to carry" or "to bring." This root is foundational in words that involve the act of carrying, bringing, or bearing something from one place to another. Words with "fer-" often convey ideas of movement, transport, or delivery.

Vocabulary:
1. **Transfer**: To move or carry something from one place, person, or position to another.
   - *Example*: He decided to transfer his account to a different bank.
2. **Conifer**: A type of tree that bears cones and has needle-like leaves; conifers carry seeds in cones.
   - *Example*: The forest was filled with tall conifers, their pine cones scattered on the ground.
3. **Ferry**: A boat or ship that carries people and goods across a body of water.
   - *Example*: They took the ferry across the river to reach the island.
4. **Proffer**: To offer or hold out something for someone's acceptance.
   - *Example*: She proffered her hand in greeting with a warm smile.

Word Duel: Transfer vs. Ferry
Question: What's the difference between transfer and ferry?
- **Transfer** is a general term that means to move or carry something from one place to another.
- **Ferry** specifically refers to a boat that transports people and goods across a body of water.

Semantic Scale: From Movement to Offering
This scale connects terms that relate to the act of carrying, bringing, or offering something, highlighting different nuances of transportation and delivery:
1. **Transfer** – The act of moving or carrying something to another place or position.
    - *Example*: He transferred the files from his computer to a portable drive.
2. **Conifer** – A type of tree that "carries" seeds within cones, symbolizing natural transport.
    - *Example*: Conifers are essential to the ecosystem, providing seeds and shelter for wildlife.
3. **Ferry** – A vessel that carries people and goods across water.
    - *Example*: The ferry arrived promptly, ready to take passengers across the bay.
4. **Proffer** – To extend or offer something for acceptance.
    - *Example*: He proffered his assistance to help her with the project.

Language Time Travel: The Origin of "Fer-"
The root "fer-" originates from the Latin word *ferre*, meaning "to carry" or "to bring." In ancient societies, the ability to carry or transport items was essential for trade, communication, and connectivity. Over time, the root *fer-* evolved in various languages to represent not only the physical act of carrying but also metaphorical ideas of offering or providing. For instance, *transfer* came to mean moving something to a

new place, while *ferry* became the term for boats that carry passengers. Words like *proffer* extended this concept to gestures of goodwill, symbolizing an offer or presentation. As language developed, words containing *fer-* preserved the timeless importance of transportation, movement, and offering within human interaction.

Story: The Journey of "Fer-"

In ancient Rome, *ferre*, meaning "to carry," was integral to daily life. The movement of goods, people, and information was essential for growth and connection. From traders transferring goods to families boarding a ferry across a river, carrying was woven into the fabric of society. As centuries passed, words derived from *fer-* captured various forms of transport and offering. *Conifers* "carried" seeds in their cones, contributing to the forest's renewal, while leaders would *proffer* their help to communities in need. Each word with *fer-* reminds us of the importance of carrying, bringing, and offering—actions that continue to connect people, places, and ideas across time and space.

ROOT: "ANTHROP-" (MEANING: "HUMAN")

The root "anthrop-" comes from the Greek word *anthrōpos*, meaning "human" or "man." It reflects concepts related to human nature, behavior, and society. Words derived from "anthrop-" often emphasize aspects of humanity, our relationships with each other, or our interpretations of the human form and experience.

Vocabulary:
1. **Anthropology**: The study of human societies, cultures, and their development.
   - *Example*: She chose to major in anthropology to understand more about diverse cultures and human history.
2. **Misanthrope**: A person who dislikes or distrusts humanity.
   - *Example*: Known as a misanthrope, he preferred solitude and avoided social gatherings.
3. **Anthropomorphic**: Attributing human characteristics to animals, objects, or gods.
   - *Example*: The anthropomorphic animal characters in the cartoon talked and dressed like humans.
4. **Philanthropy**: The desire to promote the welfare of others, often expressed through charitable donations and actions.
   - *Example*: His philanthropy led him to fund

numerous educational programs for underprivileged children.

Word Duel: Anthropology vs. Anthropology

Question: What's the difference between anthropology and philanthropy?

- **Anthropology** is the scientific study of human societies, cultures, and their development.
- **Philanthropy** refers to acts of generosity or giving, intended to benefit others and promote human welfare.

From Study to Giving

This list connects terms that revolve around human nature, from understanding it to promoting human welfare:

1. **Anthropology** – The study of humans, their cultures, and societies.
   - *Example*: Anthropology provides insights into how ancient civilizations lived and interacted.
2. **Misanthrope** – Someone who has a negative view of humanity, often avoiding social interaction.
   - *Example*: The misanthrope avoided crowded areas and preferred solitude.
3. **Anthropomorphic** – Assigning human traits to non-human entities, such as animals or objects.
   - *Example*: The children's book featured anthropomorphic animals who acted like people.
4. **Philanthropy** – The desire to promote the welfare of others, often through charitable actions.
   - *Example*: Her philanthropy helped establish a new community center for local families.

Language Time Travel: The Origin of "Anthrop-"

The root "anthrop-" originates from the Greek word *anthrōpos*, meaning "human" or "man." In ancient Greek thought, understanding human nature and society was central to philosophy and knowledge. As language evolved, *anthrop-* became the root for words exploring aspects of humanity. *Anthropology* developed as a field dedicated to the scientific study of human societies and cultures, while *misanthrope* emerged to describe those who hold negative views of humanity. The idea of *anthropomorphism* allowed people to explore human traits in animals and objects, creating connections across life forms. In contrast, *philanthropy* highlighted humanity's capacity for generosity and compassion, emphasizing efforts to uplift and improve the human condition.

Story: The Exploration of Humanity

The ancient Greeks coined the term *anthrōpos* to refer to "human," sparking a curiosity about the nature and behavior of people. Over time, words derived from *anthrop-* delved into the complexities of human life. *Anthropology* grew as a field dedicated to understanding diverse cultures and societies, shedding light on what makes us human. In contrast, a *misanthrope* represented the more skeptical side, expressing doubt or mistrust in humanity. Meanwhile, *anthropomorphic* depictions allowed humans to explore familiar traits in animals and objects, enriching literature and storytelling. Finally, *philanthropy* highlighted humanity's potential for kindness, with individuals giving back to society to uplift and support others. Each word rooted in *anthrop-* reminds us of our shared qualities, challenges, and capacity to connect and care for one another across cultures and time.

ROOT: "PED-" (MEANING: "FOOT")

The root "ped-" comes from the Latin word *pes*, meaning "foot." This root is used in words related to feet, walking, or things associated with movement. Words with "ped-" often emphasize physical movement, travel, or activities involving the feet.

Vocabulary:
1. **Pedestrian**: A person who is walking, especially in an area with vehicles.
   - *Example*: The crosswalk was busy with pedestrians heading to work.
2. **Pedicure**: A cosmetic treatment for the feet and toenails.
   - *Example*: She went to the spa for a relaxing pedicure after a long week.
3. **Pedal**: A foot-operated lever or control, often used in vehicles and musical instruments.
   - *Example*: She pressed down on the pedal to accelerate the car.
4. **Impede**: To obstruct or hinder progress, as if "getting in the way" of movement.
   - *Example*: The fallen tree impeded their path, forcing them to take a detour.

Word Duel: Pedicure vs. Pedestrian

Question: What's the difference between pedicure and pedestrian?
- **Pedicure** is a cosmetic treatment for feet, focusing on cleaning and beautifying the toenails and skin.
- **Pedestrian** refers to a person walking on foot, particularly along roads or sidewalks.

Semantic Scale: From Walking to Blocking

This scale connects terms related to feet and movement, highlighting different aspects of travel, care, and obstruction:

1. **Pedestrian** – A person who travels on foot, especially in a public space with vehicles.
    - *Example*: Pedestrians waited for the signal to cross the busy street.
2. **Pedicure** – A treatment focused on the care and appearance of feet and toenails.
    - *Example*: She enjoyed a soothing pedicure to relieve her tired feet.
3. **Pedal** – A foot-operated control used in various tools, vehicles, or instruments.
    - *Example*: The musician tapped the pedal to adjust the piano's tone.
4. **Impede** – To block or slow down progress, often by getting in the way.
    - *Example*: Construction work on the road impeded traffic for hours.

Language Time Travel: The Origin of "Ped-"

The root "ped-" comes from the Latin word *pes*, meaning "foot." In ancient times, walking was the primary mode of travel, and feet were central to daily life. As language evolved, *ped-* developed into words that focused on movement, control, and obstacles. *Pedestrian* became a term for people traveling on foot, especially in urban settings. The concept of *pedicure* grew as a form of self-care for feet, important for those who walked long distances. *Pedal* provided a way to control vehicles and musical instruments using foot pressure, highlighting the versatility of feet in diverse activities. Lastly, *impede* emerged to describe anything that "gets in the way" of movement, metaphorically blocking progress.

Story: The Path of "Ped-"

In ancient Rome, roads were bustling with people traveling on foot, giving rise to the word *pedestrian* to describe those navigating city streets. Over time, taking care of feet became essential for health, leading to the concept of *pedicure* as a form of foot care and relaxation. As technology advanced, feet were used in new ways, like pressing a *pedal* to control vehicles and instruments. Yet obstacles arose, as barriers and disruptions often *impeded* smooth travel. Each word rooted in *ped-* reflects our reliance on our feet to move forward, adapt, and overcome challenges along the journey.

ROOT: "HYDRA-" (MEANING: "WATER")

The root "hydra-" comes from the Greek word *hydōr*, meaning "water." This root appears in words that deal with water, moisture, and the essential nature of hydration. Words with "hydra-" often emphasize the presence, flow, or need for water.

Vocabulary:
1. **Hydrate**: To supply or absorb water; to maintain water balance.
   - *Example*: It's essential to hydrate during exercise to stay energized.
2. **Hydrology**: The scientific study of water, including its distribution, movement, and properties.
   - *Example*: Hydrology helps scientists understand water cycles and predict floods.
3. **Dehydration**: The condition of losing more water than is taken in, leading to a lack of moisture in the body.
   - *Example*: Symptoms of dehydration include dizziness and dry skin.
4. **Hydrant**: A pipe or fixture with a nozzle for drawing water, especially for firefighting purposes.
   - *Example*: The fire hydrant provided water to extinguish the blaze quickly.

Word Duel: Hydrate vs. Dehydration

Question: What's the difference between hydrate and dehydration?
- **Hydrate** means to add or absorb water, helping to maintain moisture.
- **Dehydration** refers to the loss of water, often leading to a lack of necessary moisture.

From Water Study to Water Supply

This list connects terms related to water, highlighting different aspects of hydration, study, and availability:

1. **Hydrology** – The study of water's properties, movement, and effects on Earth.
    - *Example*: Hydrology is crucial for understanding groundwater resources.
2. **Hydrate** – To add or maintain water content in the body or another substance.
    - *Example*: Drinking water helps you stay hydrated on hot days.
3. **Dehydration** – The condition of lacking sufficient water or moisture.
    - *Example*: Dehydration can cause fatigue and headaches.
4. **Hydrant** – A fixture for drawing water, especially during emergencies like fires.
    - *Example*: The firefighter connected the hose to the hydrant to access water.

Language Time Travel: The Origin of "Hydra-"

The root "hydra-" derives from the Greek word *hydōr*, meaning "water." Ancient societies depended on water sources for survival, and understanding its behavior and properties became essential. Over time, words using *hydra-* branched out to cover the many roles water plays in life. *Hydrology* developed as a scientific field to study water in nature, while *hydrate* came to represent the body's need for water. *Dehydration* highlighted the risks of water loss, and *hydrant* emerged as a tool for delivering water to fight fires. Each word with *hydra-* reflects our vital connection to water, from physical health to environmental understanding.

Story: The Lifeline of "Hydra-"

For ancient civilizations, water was a precious resource essential for life. This reverence for water led to the root *hydra-*, capturing the essence of moisture and its many roles. Scientists studying *hydrology* sought to unlock the mysteries of water cycles and resources, while people recognized the importance of staying *hydrated* for health and energy. Over time, the need for a water supply in emergencies led to the creation of the *hydrant*, ready to deliver water quickly. Yet, when water is scarce, *dehydration* reminds us of the risks that come with a lack of this essential resource. Words rooted in *hydra-* connect us to the fundamental need for water in sustaining life and health.

ROOT: "CAPIT-" (MEANING: "HEAD")

The root "capit-" originates from the Latin word *caput*, meaning "head." This root is central to words that refer to leadership, important positions, or the top part of something. Words with "capit-" often involve concepts of hierarchy, leadership, and prominence.

Vocabulary:
1. **Decapitate**: To remove the head, typically in a literal sense but can be used metaphorically to mean removing leadership.
    - *Example*: In historical contexts, to decapitate a ruler was often to end their reign violently.
2. **Capital**: The main city or seat of government; also, a primary or important asset, especially in finance.
    - *Example*: Washington, D.C., is the capital of the United States.
3. **Capitation**: A fee or tax levied per person, often as a headcount or poll tax.
    - *Example*: The government imposed a capitation tax to raise revenue from each individual.
4. **Captain**: The person who leads a team, ship, or group, often viewed as the "head" of the group.
    - *Example*: The captain directed the team with confidence and skill.

Word Duel: Decapitate vs. Captain

Question: What's the difference between decapitate and captain?

- **Decapitate** means to remove the head, often implying a drastic or violent action.
- **Captain** refers to a leader or head of a group, such as a ship's crew or a sports team.

Semantic Scale: From Leading to Removing the Head

This scale connects terms associated with leadership, authority, and the concept of "head," highlighting the significance of prominence and command:

1. **Captain** – The head or leader of a team, group, or ship.
    - *Example*: The captain guided the team through a difficult match.
2. **Capital** – The main city of a country or a primary asset in finance, symbolizing importance.
    - *Example*: The nation's capital hosts many government institutions.
3. **Capitation** – A tax or fee assessed per person, often calculated by headcount.
    - *Example*: The healthcare system adopted a capitation model for services.
4. **Decapitate** – To remove the head, used both literally and metaphorically to signify removal of leadership.
    - *Example*: In the story, the rebels attempted to decapitate the tyrant's rule by overthrowing him.

Language Time Travel: The Origin of "Capit-"

The root "capit-" stems from the Latin word *caput*, meaning "head." In early societies, the head was often symbolic of leadership and authority. Over time, words with *capit-* expanded in meaning. *Captain* arose as the term for a leader, whether on a ship or team, while *capital* became associated with primary cities or financial assets. *Capitation* originated as a form of head tax, charged per individual. *Decapitate*, meaning "to remove the head," highlighted the concept of losing leadership or the top of something. Words with *capit-* remind us of the importance of the head as a symbol of control, value, and position in both literal and figurative contexts.

Story: The Legacy of "Capit-"

In ancient Rome, *caput*, or "head," symbolized authority, leadership, and status. Those in power were seen as the "head" of their communities, responsible for guidance and direction. Over time, *captain* became a term for those leading teams or crews, trusted to navigate challenges. *Capital* cities emerged as the heads of nations, central to politics and culture, while financial *capital* symbolized the assets needed for growth. As the idea of individual contribution grew, *capitation* became a way to tax or count people. Finally, *decapitate* represented a dramatic severance from leadership. Each word with *capit-* preserves the legacy of the head as a symbol of prominence, authority, and influence.

ROOT: "SAN-" (MEANING: "HEALTH")

The root "san-" comes from the Latin word *sanus*, meaning "healthy" or "sound." This root appears in words related to health, wellness, and mental or physical soundness. Words derived from "san-" often focus on the state of being well, both physically and mentally.

Vocabulary:
1. **Sanity**: The condition of having a sound mind or being mentally healthy.
   - *Example*: After a stressful week, she sought some peace to regain her sanity.
2. **Sanitize**: To clean or disinfect something to make it free from germs or dirt, ensuring health and safety.
   - *Example*: It's important to sanitize the kitchen counters after preparing raw meat.
3. **Sanatorium**: A medical facility for the treatment of people with chronic illnesses, especially for those with tuberculosis or mental health conditions.
   - *Example*: In the early 20th century, many people with tuberculosis spent months in a sanatorium to recover.
4. **Sane**: Mentally healthy, rational, or able to think and behave in a reasonable way.
   - *Example*: Despite the chaos around her, she remained

calm and sane throughout the situation.

Word Duel: Sanitize vs. Sanatorium

Question: What's the difference between sanitize and sanatorium?

- **Sanitize** means to clean and disinfect something to ensure it is free from germs or harmful substances.
- **Sanatorium** is a medical institution where people receive treatment for long-term illnesses or conditions, often related to mental or physical health.

From Health to Healing

This scale connects terms related to health, focusing on mental wellness, cleanliness, and recovery:

1. **Sanity** – The state of being mentally healthy and rational.
   - *Example*: He struggled to maintain his sanity amidst the chaos of the situation.
2. **Sane** – Describes someone who is mentally healthy and rational.
   - *Example*: She was deemed sane after her evaluation by the doctors.
3. **Sanitize** – To cleanse or disinfect something to remove harmful bacteria or germs.
   - *Example*: Make sure to sanitize your hands before eating.
4. **Sanatorium** – A facility for the treatment and recovery of patients with long-term health issues.
   - *Example*: She spent several months at the sanatorium to recover from her illness.

Language Time Travel: The Origin of "San-"

The root "san-" comes from the Latin word *sanus*, meaning "healthy" or "sound." In early Latin and subsequent languages, the concept of health was tied to being "sound" in mind and body. Over time, this root evolved into words focused on maintaining or restoring health. *Sanity* emerged to describe mental health, while *sane* referred to individuals who were mentally well. *Sanitize* developed as a way to ensure cleanliness, a key element in preventing illness. *Sanatorium* came into use as a place dedicated to recovery, particularly for long-term conditions. Words with *san-* continue to emphasize the importance of health and soundness in both body and mind.

Story: The Pursuit of "San-"

In ancient times, the idea of health was often associated with being "sound" or "whole." The word *sanus* was used to describe both physical and mental well-being. As societies grew, the need for places of healing led to the establishment of *sanatoriums*, where people could recover from chronic illnesses. Over time, the practice of *sanitizing* became essential to prevent the spread of disease, especially as understanding of hygiene and cleanliness grew. The concept of *sanity* also took root, as mental well-being became recognized as crucial for overall health. Each word rooted in *san-* highlights the ongoing human pursuit of maintaining and restoring health in various forms.

ROOT: "RECT-" (MEANING: "STRAIGHT" OR "RIGHT")

The root "rect-" comes from the Latin word *rectus*, meaning "straight" or "right." This root is used in words related to things that are straight, upright, or correct in direction or moral quality. Words derived from "rect-" often involve correction, alignment, or moral integrity.

Vocabulary:
1. **Correct**: To make something free from errors or to set something right.
    - *Example*: Please correct the mistakes in your essay before submitting it.
2. **Rectify**: To correct or fix something, especially errors or problems.
    - *Example*: The technician worked hard to rectify the issue with the broken machine.
3. **Direction**: The course along which someone or something moves, or the guidance provided to reach a goal.
    - *Example*: He asked for directions to the nearest gas station.
4. **Rectangle**: A four-sided shape with straight sides and four right angles, typically with unequal adjacent

sides.
- *Example*: The table had a rectangular shape, making it perfect for the dining room.

Word Duel: Rectify vs. Correct
Question: What's the difference between rectify and correct?
- **Rectify** means to make something right or correct, often used for fixing an error or problem that has occurred.
- **Correct** simply means to remove errors or make something right, without necessarily implying that a problem has been fixed.

Semantic Scale: From Right to Shape
This scale connects terms related to straightness, correctness, and direction, emphasizing the concept of alignment and accuracy:
1. **Correct** – To make something accurate or free from errors.
    - *Example*: The teacher asked the students to correct their answers.
2. **Rectify** – To fix or correct something, often a mistake or error.
    - *Example*: After realizing the mistake, the manager took immediate steps to rectify the situation.
3. **Direction** – The path or guidance that leads to a goal, often related to movement or travel.
    - *Example*: She needed clear directions to find the new restaurant.
4. **Rectangle** – A geometric shape with four straight sides and four right angles.
    - *Example*: The room was decorated with a large rectangular rug in the center.

Language Time Travel: The Origin of "Rect-"
The root "rect-" comes from the Latin word *rectus*, meaning "straight" or "right." In Latin, *rectus* was used to describe

things that were upright, morally correct, or aligned in the right way. As the language evolved, so did the use of *rect-* in various words. *Correct* emerged to describe the act of setting things right, both in terms of accuracy and morality. *Rectify* followed as a term for the correction of mistakes or problems. *Direction* began to take on its meaning of guiding someone or something along the right path, while *rectangle* was coined as a geometric shape that was straight and aligned at right angles. These words all reflect the importance of straightness, accuracy, and proper alignment in our physical, moral, and intellectual lives.

Story: The Journey of "Rect-"

The concept of straightness and correctness has always been crucial in human societies, whether in terms of morality, measurement, or direction. The Latin root *rectus* captured this idea, giving rise to words that focused on making things right or following the correct path. *Correct* was used to describe both the process of making something accurate and the moral integrity of individuals. *Rectify* became a term for fixing errors, and *direction* emerged as a means of guiding people on the right course. The geometric term *rectangle* was coined to describe a shape with four straight sides and right angles, emphasizing clarity and precision. Together, these words show how essential straightness, alignment, and correction are in both our physical and ethical worlds.

ROOT: "MUT-" (MEANING: "CHANGE")

The root "mut-" comes from the Latin word *mutare*, meaning "to change." This root is found in words that involve alteration, transformation, or the ability to change in form or condition. Words derived from "mut-" often express the idea of change, whether in biology, behavior, or other contexts.

Vocabulary:
1. **Mutate**: To undergo a change, often in a genetic or biological context, altering form or structure.
   - *Example*: The virus can mutate, making it harder to develop a vaccine.
2. **Mutation**: The process or result of a change in the genetic material of an organism, which can lead to a new characteristic or trait.
   - *Example*: The mutation in the gene caused the plant to develop purple flowers instead of red.
3. **Immutable**: Not subject to change; unchanging over time.
   - *Example*: The laws of nature are considered immutable, remaining the same over centuries.
4. **Commute**: To travel regularly between two places, often changing locations daily (commuting to work). It can also mean to change a punishment to a less severe one.

- *Example*: He commutes from the suburbs to the city every day for work.

Word Duel: Mutate vs. Immutable

Question: What's the difference between mutate and immutable?

- **Mutate** means to change or undergo a transformation, often in a biological sense.
- **Immutable** refers to something that cannot be changed, remaining constant or fixed over time.

From Change to Permanence

This list connects terms related to change and transformation, from alterations in form to unchanging states:

1. **Mutate** – To change or alter, especially in a biological or genetic context.

   Example: The gene mutation caused the species to adapt to the new environment.

2. **Mutation** – A change or alteration, particularly in genetics, that results in a new characteristic.

   Example: A mutation in the DNA caused the fish to develop a new color pattern.

3. **Commute** – To travel regularly between two locations or to change a situation, often referring to traveling or reducing a punishment.

   Example: Many employees commute to the office every morning.

4. **Immutable** – Unchanging; not subject to alteration.

   Example: The immutable laws of physics govern the universe.

Language Time Travel: The Origin of "Mut-"

The root "mut-" derives from the Latin verb *mutare*, meaning "to change." This concept of change was vital in understanding everything from the natural world to the workings of human society. Over time, words incorporating "mut-" began to reflect various forms of change. *Mutate* and *mutation* captured changes in biological and genetic contexts, while *immutable* emerged to describe things that resist change, such as laws or certain properties. *Commute* was derived from the idea of regular changes in location, emphasizing routine shifts. These words all reflect the ongoing process of transformation, alteration, and consistency.

The Power of "Mut-"

Change is a constant force in life, from the evolution of species to the way we move through the world. The root *mut-* speaks to this fundamental concept of transformation. In biology, *mutate* describes the process by which organisms change over generations, often leading to new traits through *mutation*. On the other hand, some things remain constant, and *immutable* was coined to describe those unchanging elements of nature or law. *Commute* also draws on the idea of movement or change in location, something many people experience daily. Whether embracing change or maintaining stability, words with *mut-* highlight the power of transformation in shaping the world around us.

ROOT: "MORT-" (MEANING: "DEATH")

The root "mort-" comes from the Latin word *mors*, meaning "death." This root appears in words related to death, dying, or the concept of life and death. Words derived from "mort-" often involve the inevitability of death or the condition of being subject to it, as well as the idea of being beyond death.

Vocabulary:
1. **Mortality**: The condition of being subject to death; the death rate within a population.
   - *Example*: The mortality rate in the region has decreased due to improvements in healthcare.
2. **Immortal**: Not subject to death; living forever.
   - *Example*: In Greek mythology, the gods were immortal, living for eternity without aging or dying.
3. **Mortal**: Subject to death; human or earthly, in contrast to divine or eternal.
   - *Example*: Even the greatest kings are mortal and eventually pass away.
4. **Mortuary**: A place where bodies are stored or prepared for burial; a funeral home.
   - *Example*: After the accident, the bodies were taken to the local mortuary for identification.

Word Duel: Mortal vs. Immortal
Question: What's the difference between mortal and

immortal?
- **Mortal** means subject to death; humans and other living beings are mortal, meaning they will eventually die.
- **Immortal** means not subject to death; something or someone that lives forever, often used for gods or legendary figures.

Semantic Scale: From Death to Eternity
This scale connects terms related to life, death, and eternity, emphasizing the transient nature of life versus the concept of immortality:

1. **Mortal** – Subject to death; human beings are mortal, meaning they will eventually die.

Example: The mortal lives of the villagers were marked by hard work and community spirit.

2. **Mortality** – The condition of being mortal; refers to death rates or the inevitability of death.

Example: The high mortality rate during the war was a tragic consequence of the conflict.

3. **Mortuary** – A facility for the storage and preparation of bodies after death.

Example: The mortuary was filled with mourners and families making arrangements.

4. **Immortal** – Not subject to death; eternal or everlasting.

Example: The ancient myth spoke of an immortal being who could never die.

Language Time Travel: The Origin of "Mort-"
The root "mort-" comes from the Latin word *mors*, meaning "death." In ancient cultures, death was a key concept, and many myths and stories revolved around the question of mortality and immortality. Words like *mortal* and *mortality* emerged to describe the human condition—finite, fragile, and subject to death. The term *immortal* was coined to express the idea of eternal life,

often attributed to gods, heroes, and legends. *Mortuary* was developed to refer to places associated with the dead, where bodies were prepared for burial. These words reflect humanity's fascination with life and death and the eternal struggle to understand the inevitability of death.

Cycle of "Mort-"

Death is a fundamental aspect of the human experience, and the root *mort-* has captured this reality for centuries. Ancient cultures sought to understand death, and thus, words like *mortal* and *mortality* came into use to describe human life as fleeting and temporary. In contrast, immortality was a concept embraced by myths, with gods and heroes often portrayed as being *immortal*, beyond the reach of death. *Mortuary* was established as a place to care for the dead, as the practice of burial and mourning became an essential part of societies. Over time, these words grew into expressions of our relationship with death, highlighting both its inevitability and the desire for eternity.

ROOT: "MONO-" (MEANING: "ONE" OR "SINGLE")

The root "mono-" comes from the Greek word *monos*, meaning "one" or "single." It is used in words that refer to something being singular, unified, or consisting of one element. Words derived from "mono-" often involve the idea of singularity, uniformity, or dominance.

Vocabulary:
1. **Monologue**: A long speech or talk by one person, often in a play, movie, or conversation.
   - *Example*: The actor's monologue was so powerful that it moved the entire audience to tears.
2. **Monotone**: A continuous, unchanging tone of voice, lacking variation in pitch or emotion.
   - *Example*: The lecturer's monotone delivery made it hard to stay focused during the class.
3. **Monopoly**: A situation where one company or entity controls an entire market or product, eliminating competition.
   - *Example*: The tech giant's monopoly on smartphone sales has been challenged by smaller companies.
4. **Monolithic**: Describing something that is large, uniform, and indivisible; often used to describe large, imposing structures or organizations.
   - *Example*: The corporation had a monolithic

structure, with no room for independent decision-making.

Word Duel: Monologue vs. Monotone

Question: What's the difference between monologue and monotone?

- **Monologue** refers to a speech or performance by one person, often long or uninterrupted.
- **Monotone** refers to a speech or voice that lacks variation in pitch, tone, or emotion, often sounding flat or dull.

From One to Dominance

This list connects terms related to singularity, unity, and control, emphasizing different aspects of being one or having a singular focus:

1. **Monologue** – A long speech delivered by one person, often expressing personal thoughts or emotions.
   - *Example*: The actor performed a dramatic monologue that left the audience spellbound.
2. **Monotone** – A voice or sound that remains flat, without variation in pitch or intonation.
   - *Example*: His monotone voice made the news report sound less exciting.
3. **Monopoly** – A market or situation where one entity dominates or controls all aspects of a particular industry or resource.
   - *Example*: The company's monopoly on electric car batteries made it nearly impossible for competitors to enter the market.
4. **Monolithic** – Describing something that is singular and unified, often on a large scale, with no variation or flexibility.
   - *Example*: The monolithic building stood like a fortress in the center of the city.

Language Time Travel: The Origin of "Mono-"

The root "mono-" comes from the Greek word *monos*, meaning "one" or "single." In ancient Greece, the concept of unity and singularity was often discussed in philosophical and mathematical contexts, leading to the development of words that referred to singular entities. *Monologue* emerged as a way to describe a speech or performance delivered by one person, often expressing their thoughts or emotions. *Monotone* followed to describe a sound or voice that remains unchanged, lacking variation. *Monopoly* originated from the Greek word for "one seller," referring to a market controlled by a single entity. *Monolithic* described structures or systems that were large, solid, and unified, often without flexibility or change.

Story: The Power of One

In a small town, there was a public speech event where the mayor, a man known for his *monotone* voice, delivered a *monologue* about the future of the town. His voice, flat and unchanging, echoed through the hall, but the crowd remained unmoved, as his lack of inflection made it hard for anyone to feel his passion.

However, the mayor's words weren't just about a simple town development plan. He announced the construction of a *monolithic* structure that would dominate the town's skyline: a massive, towering building that would house his new business empire. The project was set to solidify his control over every major industry in the area. The more people talked, the more it became clear that the mayor was slowly creating a *monopoly*, where only his businesses would thrive, and competition would be silenced.

Despite the lack of enthusiasm from the crowd, the mayor's vision of singularity and control was already in motion, and soon, nothing in the town would be able to compete with the power of his *monolithic* empire.

ROOT: "MIGR-" (MEANING: "MOVE")

The root "migr-" comes from the Latin word *migrare*, meaning "to move" or "to change place." This root is found in words that relate to movement, especially the movement of people, animals, or things from one place to another. Words derived from "migr-" often describe the act of traveling, relocating, or the people involved in such movements.

Vocabulary:
1. **Migrate**: To move from one place to another, especially regularly or seasonally.
   - *Example*: Birds migrate south for the winter to escape the cold weather.
2. **Immigration**: The process of coming to live permanently in a foreign country.
   - *Example*: The country has strict immigration laws that make it difficult for people to settle there.
3. **Emigrant**: A person who leaves their own country to settle permanently in another.
   - *Example*: My grandfather was an emigrant from Italy who moved to the United States in the early 1900s.
4. **Migrant**: A person or animal that moves from one place to another, often in search of work or better living conditions.
   - *Example*: Migrant workers travel across the country

during harvest season to find employment.

Word Duel: Emigrant vs. Immigrant

Question: What's the difference between an emigrant and an immigrant?

- **Emigrant** refers to someone who leaves their own country to live in another.
- **Immigrant** refers to someone who moves into a new country to live there permanently. Essentially, an emigrant leaves, and an immigrant arrives.

Semantic Scale: From Moving to Relocation

This scale connects terms related to the movement of people and things, from traveling or moving temporarily to the idea of permanent relocation:

1. **Migrate** – To move, often seasonally or temporarily, to a new location.
   - *Example*: Many species of fish migrate upstream to spawn during certain seasons.
2. **Migrant** – A person or animal who moves from one place to another, often for work or better opportunities.
   - *Example*: Migrant farm workers follow the harvest from state to state in search of seasonal jobs.
3. **Emigrant** – A person who leaves their homeland to settle in another country permanently.
   - *Example*: The emigrants from Eastern Europe made a new home in the United States in the late 19th century.
4. **Immigration** – The act of moving into a new country with the intention to settle there permanently.
   - *Example*: The United States has a long history of immigration, with people from all over the world seeking a better life.

Language Time Travel: The Origin of "Migr-"

The root "migr-" comes from the Latin *migrare*, which

means "to move" or "to change place." In ancient times, the movement of people was often in search of better living conditions, food, or opportunities. Over time, words like *migrate* and *immigration* came into use to describe the journey of individuals or groups from one place to another. As transportation improved and migration patterns became more regular, terms like *emigrant* and *migrant* emerged to describe those moving from one country or region to another. These words continue to reflect the human experience of movement, seeking new opportunities, or escaping hardship.

Story: A Journey of Hope

Marco and Elena, an Italian couple from a small village, decided to *migrate* to America in search of a better life. As *emigrants*, they left behind their home and sailed across the Atlantic, driven by the hope of a brighter future. Upon arriving in New York City, they became part of the wave of *immigrants* seeking new opportunities.

Though life was challenging, Marco found work, and Elena helped fellow *migrants* settle in. Over the years, their hard work paid off, and their children thrived in their new home. They realized that their journey had not only changed their lives but had become a part of the greater story of *immigration* in America.

In the end, Marco and Elena's decision to *migrate* was a testament to resilience and the pursuit of a better life.

ROOT: "LEV-" (MEANING: "LIGHT" OR "LIFT")

The root "lev-" comes from the Latin word *levare*, which means "to lift" or "to make light." This root is found in words that relate to lightness, elevation, or lifting up. Words derived from "lev-" often describe things that are light in weight, actions that lift or elevate, or qualities that are cheerful or lighthearted.

Vocabulary:
1. **Levitate**: To rise or cause to rise and float in the air, often seemingly without support.
   - *Example*: The magician made the ball levitate above his hand during the performance.
2. **Elevate**: To lift something to a higher position or raise it up.
   - *Example*: The new promotion will elevate her career to the next level.
3. **Leverage**: To use something to its maximum advantage, often referring to a financial or strategic advantage.
   - *Example*: By using their financial leverage, they were able to negotiate a better deal.
4. **Levity**: Lightness or humor, especially when inappropriate or lacking seriousness.
   - *Example*: His levity during the serious meeting

caused some people to feel uncomfortable.

Word Duel: Levitate vs. Elevate

Question: What's the difference between levitate and elevate?

- **Levitate** refers specifically to rising or floating in the air, often without any visible support. It often implies a magical or supernatural force.
- **Elevate** refers to lifting something to a higher position, but it doesn't imply that it will float or remain in the air. It's a more general term for raising something physically or metaphorically.

From Lightness to Lifting

This list connects terms related to lightness and lifting, from something floating lightly to lifting with effort:

1. **Levity** – Lightness or humor, especially in a situation that calls for seriousness.
    - *Example*: His levity during the crisis made everyone think he wasn't taking things seriously.
2. **Levitate** – To rise or cause to rise and float, often implying defying gravity or being lifted without support.
    - *Example*: The yoga instructor demonstrated how to levitate your body using controlled breathing techniques.
3. **Elevate** – To raise something to a higher level, physically or metaphorically.
    - *Example*: The charity event helped elevate awareness for the cause.
4. **Leverage** – Using something to gain an advantage or lift yourself up, often in a strategic or financial context.
    - *Example*: She used her expertise in the industry to leverage her position and gain more clients.

Language Time Travel: The Origin of "Lev-"

The root "lev-" originates from the Latin *levare*, meaning "to lift" or "to lighten." In ancient times, lifting or raising something often signified a physical act of making something lighter or elevating it in status or position. Over time, this idea expanded beyond physical actions to include metaphorical uses such as elevating one's status or leveraging resources for advantage. As society advanced, the concept of lightness also grew to encompass both the physical lightness of objects and the more abstract idea of humor and ease, reflected in words like levity.

Story: A Lifted Spirit

Sarah had always dreamed of being more than just an office worker. One day, a friend offered her the chance to work on a major project that would elevate her career. She was excited and nervous, but she knew it was an opportunity she couldn't pass up. As she worked on the project, Sarah began to feel lighter in spirit, as if her hard work was making her rise above the challenges. Her success on the project led to a promotion, and soon, she was able to leverage her new position to help others. Her journey was one of elevation—lifting herself and her team to new heights of achievement.

In the end, Sarah realized that it wasn't just about lifting herself but about uplifting those around her, creating a team full of positive energy and success.

ROOT: "LAT-" (MEANING: "SIDE" OR "WIDE")

The root "lat-" comes from the Latin word *latus*, meaning "wide" or "side." This root appears in words that describe things related to width, side, or direction. Words derived from "lat-" often refer to physical sides, perspectives, or a range of degrees.

Vocabulary:
1. **Latitude**: The distance north or south of the equator, measured in degrees. It can also refer to freedom of action or thought.
   - *Example*: The latitude of the city's location made it experience mild winters.
2. **Bilateral**: Involving two sides or parties, especially in agreements or relationships.
   - *Example*: The two countries signed a bilateral trade agreement to improve economic relations.
3. **Collateral**: Something pledged as security for repayment of a loan or as additional support. It can also refer to things that are side by side or secondary.
   - *Example*: He offered his car as collateral for the business loan.
4. **Lateral**: Relating to or situated at the side of something; moving sideways.
   - *Example*: The lateral movement of the ship caused it

to drift off course.

Word Duel: Bilateral vs. Lateral

Question: What's the difference between bilateral and lateral?
- **Bilateral** refers to something involving two sides, parties, or groups, often in the context of agreements or relationships.
- **Lateral** refers to something that is related to or situated at the side of something, especially in terms of physical movement or position.

Semantic Scale: From Side to Wide

This scale connects terms related to sides, from the specific direction to a broader range:

1. **Lateral** – Refers to the side or something moving sideways.

   Example: The lateral shift in the market showed how companies were adjusting to new consumer trends.

2. **Collateral** – Something secondary or side by side, often used to refer to support or security in financial contexts.

   Example: The bank required collateral to back the loan.

3. **Bilateral** – Involving two sides or parties, especially in the context of negotiations or agreements.

   Example: The two countries agreed to a bilateral pact on environmental protection.

4. **Latitude** – Refers to freedom, scope, or range, often used to describe both geographic location and the extent of freedom of action.

   Example: The manager gave her team a lot of latitude in how they handled the project.

Language Time Travel: The Origin of "Lat-"

The root "lat-" comes from the Latin *latus*, meaning "wide" or "side." In ancient times, the idea of width or side was significant in both physical and metaphorical terms. From geographical latitude to the lateral movement of armies, the concept of "lat-" has influenced how we discuss space, direction, and relationships. Over time, words like collateral and bilateral evolved, reflecting a shift from physical descriptions to more abstract uses, such as freedom of action or agreements between two parties.

Story: A Wide Path Ahead

David and Anna had always dreamed of starting a business together. After years of planning, they decided to create a bilateral partnership, where each would bring their strengths to the table. They agreed on collateral terms to secure their initial investment, and with their business plan in hand, they set off on their new venture. As the business grew, they began to see the importance of lateral thinking—being open to different perspectives and approaches.   Their partnership thrived because they understood the value of both a wide range of possibilities and the focused, side-by-side teamwork that kept them aligned.

In the end, David and Anna's venture succeeded because they navigated the balance between latitude for creativity and the clear, bilateral agreement that guided their journey.

ROOT: "JOV-" (MEANING: "JUPITER" OR "GOOD")

The root "jov-" comes from the Latin word *Iuppiter* (Jupiter), the king of the gods in Roman mythology. Jupiter was often associated with joy, good fortune, and positive energy. Words derived from "jov-" typically relate to joy, good cheer, or happiness, as well as things that are of a positive or joyful nature.

Vocabulary:
1. **Jovial**: Cheerful and good-natured, full of high spirits.
   - *Example*: The jovial atmosphere at the party made everyone feel welcome and happy.
2. **Joviality**: The state or quality of being cheerful, good-humored, or full of joy.
   - *Example*: Her joviality was contagious, and soon everyone was smiling and laughing.
3. **Jove**: An alternative name for Jupiter, often used to refer to the Roman god or the planet. It can also refer to a source of good fortune or happiness.
   - *Example*: The gods smiled upon their journey, and they felt as though Jove himself was guiding them.
4. **Enjoy**: To take pleasure in something, to have a positive experience or feeling of satisfaction.
   - *Example*: We enjoyed the concert so much that we

stayed for the entire show.

Word Duel: Jovial vs. Enjoy
Question: What's the difference between jovial and enjoy?
- **Jovial** refers to a cheerful, happy, and good-natured personality or atmosphere. It's a description of someone's demeanor or the mood of an event.
- **Enjoy** refers to actively experiencing or taking pleasure in something. It's about the act of finding joy or satisfaction in an experience.

From Joyful to Enjoying
This list connects terms related to happiness and enjoyment, from a cheerful mood to the active experience of joy:

1. **Jovial** – Full of cheer and good humor, often describing a person or the mood of an event.
Example: His jovial personality made him the life of the party.
2. **Joviality** – The quality of being jovial, a state of joyfulness or cheerfulness.
Example: Her joviality spread through the room like sunshine, lifting everyone's spirits.
3. **Jove** – Refers to the Roman god of joy and good fortune, or metaphorically to good luck or happiness.
Example: It felt as though Jove had granted them the perfect weather for their wedding day.
4. **Enjoy** – To take pleasure or satisfaction in something, to actively experience joy.
Example: They enjoyed their vacation by exploring new places and trying new foods.

Language Time Travel: The Origin of "Jov-"
The root "jov-" comes from *Iuppiter* (Jupiter), the Roman god of the sky and thunder, associated with good fortune, happiness, and the well-being of people. Jupiter's connection to joy and abundance influenced the evolution of words like jovial, which describes a joyful personality or atmosphere, and enjoy, which

describes the active experience of happiness. Over time, these words have come to symbolize not just literal joy, but also a positive outlook and enjoyment of life.

Story: A Jovial Gathering

It was the holiday season, and the family gathered for their annual reunion. The air was filled with joviality, as laughter echoed from every corner of the house. Uncle Bob, always the life of the party, was telling jokes, and his jovial nature made everyone smile. Even the children, who had been a bit grumpy before, couldn't help but enjoy the warmth of the family's laughter. As they sat around the table, enjoying a delicious feast, it felt as though the gods themselves were smiling down, filling the room with joy and good fortune.

By the end of the night, everyone agreed it had been one of the most joyful gatherings they'd ever had, a true celebration of togetherness.

ROOT: "IGN-" (MEANING: "FIRE")

The root "ign-" comes from the Latin word *ignis*, meaning "fire." This root is found in words that relate to fire, heat, or burning. Words derived from "ign-" often describe actions related to starting fires, the presence of heat, or an intense passion for something.

Vocabulary:
1. **Ignite**: To start a fire or cause something to begin burning. It can also refer to sparking enthusiasm or passion.
    - *Example*: The fireworks ignited the night sky, dazzling the crowd with colors.
2. **Ignition**: The act or process of starting a fire or triggering an engine to start. It can also refer to the beginning of something, such as an idea or feeling.
    - *Example*: The ignition of the engine signaled the start of their road trip across the country.
3. **Ignis**: The Latin word for fire, often used in scientific or poetic contexts.
    - *Example*: The ancient Romans worshipped *ignis* as a symbol of energy and power.
4. **Pyromaniac**: A person with a compulsive desire to start fires, often used to describe someone with an unhealthy obsession with fire.

- *Example*: The police were investigating the town for signs of a pyromaniac after several unexplained fires broke out.

Word Duel: Ignite vs. Ignition

Question: What's the difference between ignite and ignition?

- **Ignite** refers to the act of setting something on fire or causing it to begin burning, or it can metaphorically mean sparking an emotion or idea.
- **Ignition** refers to the process or event that triggers the fire or starts something, such as the starting mechanism of a vehicle or the initial moment when something begins.

Semantic Scale: From Fire Starting to Fire-Related Activities

This scale connects terms related to fire and heat, from the starting point to actions involving fire:

1. **Ignis** – Refers to fire itself, the source of heat and combustion.

   Example: The ancient Greeks revered *ignis* as the essential element of life and energy.

2. **Ignite** – To set something on fire or to begin burning, both literally and figuratively.

   Example: His speech ignited the crowd, inspiring them to take action.

3. **Ignition** – The process or action of starting a fire or engine, often referring to a trigger or spark.

   Example: The ignition of the match was all it took to start the campfire.

4. **Pyromaniac** – A person with a compulsive desire to start fires, often in an unhealthy or dangerous way.

   Example: After years of trouble with the law, the pyromaniac was finally caught and taken into custody.

Language Time Travel: The Origin of "Ign-"

The root "ign-" comes from the Latin word *ignis*, which means "fire." In ancient times, fire was both a necessity and a powerful force, symbolizing energy, destruction, and renewal. Words like ignite and ignition grew from the idea of controlling or triggering fire, while pyromaniac developed to describe an obsessive behavior centered around fire. Over time, the root "ign-" became symbolic not just of physical fire, but also of the idea of sparking change, passion, or intensity.

Story: The Spark of Change

Marcus had always been drawn to fire. From a young age, he loved watching the flames flicker in the hearth, feeling the warmth and power of the blaze. As an adult, he channeled his fascination into a career as a firefighter. One night, while on duty, he found himself in a situation where a single spark could ignite the entire building. With quick thinking and calm precision, he activated the ignition system in the fire truck, saving the lives of many trapped inside.

But Marcus's love for fire was more than just a job—it was a metaphor for the passion that drove him. He knew that sometimes, just like fire, a small action could ignite a revolution, a change that would forever alter the course of events. His bravery on that night became a turning point for the community, much like the ignition of a powerful flame—small at first, but capable of transforming everything in its path.

ROOT: "HYPO-" (MEANING: "UNDER" OR "BELOW")

The root "hypo-" comes from the Greek word *hypo*, meaning "under" or "below." It is used in words that describe something that is beneath a certain level or under normal conditions. "Hypo-" is often used in medical and scientific terms to indicate something that is deficient, beneath a normal level, or lower than expected.

Vocabulary:
1. **Hypodermic**: Relating to or situated beneath the skin, often referring to injections or needles that go under the skin.
   - *Example*: The doctor administered a hypodermic injection to deliver the vaccine.
2. **Hypothesis**: A proposed explanation for a phenomenon, often based on limited evidence and used as a starting point for further investigation.
   - *Example*: The scientist formed a hypothesis about the effects of the new drug on heart health.
3. **Hypoglycemia**: A condition characterized by abnormally low blood sugar levels.
   - *Example*: People with diabetes need to be careful about hypoglycemia, which can cause weakness and

dizziness.
4. **Hypothermia**: A dangerous condition that occurs when the body's temperature falls below normal levels, usually due to prolonged exposure to cold.
   - *Example*: After hours of being stranded in the cold, he developed hypothermia and required immediate medical attention.

Word Duel: Hypodermic vs. Hypothermia
Question: What's the difference between hypodermic and hypothermia?
- **Hypodermic** refers to something related to or situated beneath the skin, often in the context of injections or medical procedures that involve the skin's lower layers.
- **Hypothermia** refers to a medical condition in which the body's core temperature drops below normal levels, typically due to prolonged exposure to cold environments.

Below Normal to Below the Surface
This list connects terms related to something being "under" or "below," from medical conditions to physical placement:
1. **Hypodermic** – Referring to something that is beneath the skin, such as an injection or needle.

   Example: The hypodermic needle was used to inject the vaccine just under the skin.

2. **Hypothesis** – An idea or explanation that is below the level of certainty, often tested through experiments or further research.

   Example: The hypothesis about the new treatment's effects was tested through a series of clinical trials.

3. **Hypoglycemia** – A condition where blood sugar levels are too low, which can be dangerous if not addressed.

   Example: The patient's hypoglycemia was corrected with a quick dose of sugar.

4. **Hypothermia** – A condition caused by the body's

temperature falling below normal, often due to extreme cold.

Example: After hiking in the snow for hours, they had to seek shelter to prevent hypothermia.

Language Time Travel: The Origin of "Hypo-"

The prefix "hypo-" comes from the Greek word *hypo*, meaning "under" or "below." In ancient Greek, this concept was often used to describe something beneath the surface or less than what was considered normal. Over time, it was adopted into scientific and medical terminology to describe conditions or measurements that were under a certain threshold, like hypothermia (low body temperature) or hypoglycemia (low blood sugar). The root continues to be used to refer to things that are deficient, beneath, or lower than expected.

Story: A Case of Hypothermia

Samantha had always loved outdoor adventures, but one winter hike took an unexpected turn. After losing her way in the snowstorm, her body temperature dropped dangerously low, and she began to feel weak and disoriented. Recognizing the symptoms of hypothermia, her hiking partner wrapped her in blankets and started a fire. They managed to get her warm and safe, but it was a close call.

Later, Samantha learned more about hypothermia and how essential it was to be prepared for extreme conditions. She shared her story to raise awareness, ensuring that others understood the importance of staying warm and monitoring body temperature during winter activities. Her experience was a reminder that nature's power is unpredictable, and being prepared can make all the difference in avoiding potentially dangerous situations.

ROOT: "EQUI-" (MEANING: "EQUAL")

The root "equi-" comes from the Latin word *aequus*, meaning "equal" or "level." This root appears in words that express the idea of equality, balance, fairness, or similarity. Words derived from "equi-" often emphasize the concept of things being the same or in a state of balance or fairness.

Vocabulary:
1. **Equal**: Having the same value, amount, or status; being the same in quantity or degree.
   - *Example*: All citizens should have equal rights under the law.
2. **Equilibrium**: A state of balance or stability, where opposing forces or influences are equal and counteract each other.
   - *Example*: The body maintains equilibrium to stay balanced while standing.
3. **Equity**: Fairness or justice in the way people are treated, or the value of an asset after liabilities are deducted.
   - *Example*: The company is committed to promoting equity in the workplace, ensuring that all employees have equal opportunities.
4. **Equivalent**: Equal in value, amount, function, or meaning; something that is the same or comparable

in some way.
- *Example*: A dollar in the U.S. is equivalent to around 0.85 euros in Europe.

Word Duel: Equity vs. Equivalent

Question: What's the difference between equity and equivalent?

- **Equity** refers to fairness, justice, or the value of something after debts or liabilities are subtracted. It often involves a sense of balance in how people or things are treated.
- **Equivalent** refers to something that is equal in value, amount, or function, without necessarily involving fairness or balance.

Semantic Scale: From Equality to Balance

This scale connects terms related to equality and balance, from fairness in treatment to objects or values being equal:

1. **Equal** – Referring to things that are the same in quantity, value, or status.
   Example: Everyone deserves equal opportunities regardless of background.
2. **Equilibrium** – A state of balance where opposing forces or influences are equal.
   Example: The chemical reaction reached equilibrium when the rate of forward and reverse reactions became equal.
3. **Equity** – Fairness or justice in treatment, or the value of an asset after debts have been settled.
   Example: The court's decision was based on the principles of equity and fairness.
4. **Equivalent** – Something that is equal in value, amount, or function.
   Example: A liter of water is equivalent to 1,000 milliliters.

Language Time Travel: The Origin of "Equi-"

The root "equi-" comes from the Latin word *aequus*, which

means "level," "fair," or "equal." In ancient times, the concept of balance and fairness was crucial in both legal and societal contexts. Over time, words derived from *aequus* evolved to describe not only physical balance (like equilibrium) but also fairness (like equity) and the idea of similarity (like equivalent). These terms are still used today in a wide variety of fields, from law to science, to express the importance of equality and balance in human life.

Story: A Journey Toward Equity

Amira and her team were tasked with designing a new hiring system for the company. They were determined to create a process that was fair and promoted equity, ensuring that all applicants were evaluated based on their skills and experience, not their background or personal connections. After reviewing the current process, they noticed some inequalities and made adjustments to eliminate biases, making the system more transparent and accessible.

As the new system was implemented, Amira was pleased to see that it worked. Candidates were treated equally, and the company's hiring process was much more equitable. Soon, they noticed an increase in diverse applicants and higher employee satisfaction. Amira's work was a testament to the power of equity, where equal opportunities led to a more balanced and inclusive workplace for everyone.

ROOT: "DUR-" (MEANING: "HARD" OR "LASTING")

The root "dur-" comes from the Latin word *durare*, meaning "to last" or "to endure." This root is used in words that describe things that are strong, hard, or able to last for a long time. It is also found in terms that describe the ability to withstand difficult conditions or remain intact over time.

Vocabulary:
1. **Durable**: Able to withstand wear, pressure, or damage; long-lasting.
   - *Example*: These durable boots will last for years even through harsh weather conditions.
2. **Endure**: To suffer or tolerate something difficult or unpleasant over a period of time; to last through challenges.
   - *Example*: The soldiers endured months of hardship during the battle, but they remained strong.
3. **Duration**: The length of time something lasts or continues.
   - *Example*: The duration of the movie was over two hours, so we decided to bring snacks.
4. **Indurate**: To make something hard or resistant, often in the context of emotions or physical objects.

- *Example*: The harsh environment indurated his skin, making it rough and tough.

Word Duel: Endure vs. Duration

Question: What's the difference between endure and duration?
- **Endure** refers to the ability to withstand or tolerate something difficult or painful over time.
- **Duration** refers to the length of time something continues or exists.

From Lasting to Withstanding

This list connects terms related to enduring or lasting, from the amount of time something lasts to the ability to withstand difficulty:

1. **Durable** – Able to last for a long time without breaking or wearing out, often used to describe materials or objects.

    Example: This durable backpack can survive years of use in rugged conditions.

2. **Endure** – To persist through difficult or challenging circumstances, often with a sense of struggle or suffering.

    Example: They endured the cold winter to finish the construction project on time.

3. **Duration** – The period of time during which something lasts or continues.

    Example: The duration of the flight was 12 hours, making it the longest trip they had ever taken.

4. **Indurate** – To make something hard or resistant, typically used in reference to physical objects or emotions that have become hardened by experience.

    Example: The constant pressure indurated her resolve, making her more determined than ever.

Language Time Travel: The Origin of "Dur-"

The root "dur-" originates from the Latin verb *durare*, meaning "to last" or "to endure." The concept of durability and endurance was important in ancient cultures, both in terms of physical strength and the ability to survive hardships. Over time, the root evolved to describe not just the physical toughness of objects (like durable materials) but also the emotional and mental resilience needed to endure adversity. Words like *endure* and *indurate* reflect the enduring strength required to overcome challenges or remain unchanged over time.

Story: The Endurance of the Mountain Climber

Ella had always dreamed of climbing the highest peak in the world. After years of preparation and training, she finally stood at the base of Mount Everest. The journey was grueling, and the harsh conditions tested her in ways she never imagined. But with each step, she learned to endure the cold, the altitude, and the exhaustion.

As she reached the summit, Ella realized that it wasn't just her physical strength that had gotten her there; it was her mental endurance. The duration of the climb, the long months of preparation, and the many sacrifices she had made had all led to this moment. Standing atop the world, she understood the true meaning of durability—both the mountain and her spirit had endured the test of time.

ROOT: "DUCT-" (MEANING: "LEAD" OR "CONDUCT")

The root "duct-" comes from the Latin verb *ducere*, meaning "to lead" or "to conduct." This root appears in words that refer to leading, guiding, or channeling something, whether it's physical, like directing a flow of water, or metaphorical, like guiding someone's behavior or thoughts.

Vocabulary:
1. **Conduct**: To lead or guide; also refers to how a person behaves or manages something, especially a task or responsibility.
   - *Example*: The teacher conducted the class with great skill, ensuring every student understood the lesson.
2. **Induce**: To lead or bring about a particular action, feeling, or situation; to cause something to happen.
   - *Example*: The doctor's explanation of the benefits of exercise induced a positive change in the patient's lifestyle.
3. **Aqueduct**: A structure built to lead or carry water, typically across a valley or other difficult terrain.
   - *Example*: The ancient Romans built impressive aqueducts to bring water into the city.
4. **Deduct**: To subtract or take away an amount from a

total, leading to a smaller sum.
- *Example*: The company deducted the taxes from his paycheck before he received it.

Word Duel: Deduct vs. Induce
Question: What's the difference between deduct and induce?
- **Deduct** refers to the action of taking away or subtracting something from a total amount, often in financial or mathematical contexts.
- **Induce** refers to the act of causing or leading to a particular outcome or situation, often by persuading or influencing someone.

Semantic Scale: From Leading to Changing
This scale connects terms related to leading or guiding, from physical channels to influencing or changing outcomes:
1. **Conduct** – To lead, guide, or manage something or someone.

   Example: The conductor conducted the orchestra with precision and grace.
2. **Aqueduct** – A structure used to channel or carry water from one place to another, often over a long distance.

   Example: The aqueduct system allowed ancient cities to thrive by providing a steady water supply.
3. **Induce** – To lead to or cause a specific result, typically by influencing or persuading.

   Example: The speech induced a sense of hope and motivation among the audience.
4. **Deduct** – To take away or subtract something, especially in financial contexts.

   Example: They deducted the cost of the meal from the total bill.

Language Time Travel: The Origin of "Duct-"
The root "duct-" comes from the Latin *ducere*, meaning "to lead" or "to conduct." In ancient times, the idea of leading

was important both in practical matters, like guiding water through aqueducts, and in leadership, such as guiding people through decisions or actions. Over time, the concept of leading expanded metaphorically, giving rise to words like *induce* (to lead someone to a conclusion or action) and *deduct* (to lead away or subtract). These terms reflect the many ways in which the idea of leadership or direction plays a role in both the physical and abstract aspects of life.

Story: The Leadership of the Engineer

Liam, a civil engineer, was tasked with designing a new water system for a small town. The project required building a modern aqueduct to bring fresh water from a river miles away. Despite the challenges, Liam worked tirelessly, leading his team through each stage of construction.

One day, as they faced a significant obstacle, Liam induced a breakthrough idea that led to a solution, saving both time and resources. He explained how adjusting the water flow would reduce the need for costly modifications. Thanks to his leadership and ability to guide the team through difficulties, the project was a success. The town now had access to clean water, and Liam's conduct throughout the project was praised as exemplary.

ROOT: "DEM-" (MEANING: "PEOPLE")

The root "dem-" comes from the Greek word *demos*, meaning "people" or "the population." It is used in words that refer to people, society, or the distribution and study of populations. Many words derived from "dem-" are related to governance, population health, and the structure of society.

Vocabulary:
1. **Democracy**: A system of government where power is vested in the people, either directly or through elected representatives.
   - *Example*: The citizens voted to elect leaders in the country's democracy.
2. **Demographic**: Relating to the statistical study of populations, especially with regard to age, race, income, or education.
   - *Example*: The demographic data showed a growing population of young people in the region.
3. **Epidemic**: A widespread occurrence of a particular disease or phenomenon in a population within a specific area or community.
   - *Example*: The city faced an epidemic of flu cases last winter, with many people falling ill.
4. **Pandemic**: An epidemic that has spread across a large geographic area, affecting multiple countries or

continents.
- *Example*: The COVID-19 pandemic brought global challenges, impacting millions of lives worldwide.

Word Duel: Epidemic vs. Pandemic

Question: What's the difference between epidemic and pandemic?
- **Epidemic** refers to a disease or phenomenon that is prevalent in a specific area or population, often confined to a community or country.
- **Pandemic** refers to an epidemic that has spread across multiple countries or continents, affecting a global population

Population Related Terms

This list connects terms related to the spread of disease and the study of populations, from local occurrences to global phenomena:
- **Democracy** – A system where the people have the power to govern, typically through elected representatives.
  - *Example*: The people of the country actively participated in the democracy by voting for their leaders.
- **Demographic** – Relating to the statistical characteristics of a population, like age, gender, and social status.
  - *Example*: The demographic report revealed that the city's population was becoming more diverse.
- **Epidemic** – A disease or condition affecting a large number of people in a specific area or community.
  - *Example*: The flu epidemic affected thousands in the region, leading to a health crisis.
- **Pandemic** – A global epidemic, typically affecting multiple countries and large populations across continents.
  - *Example*: The pandemic caused widespread changes in how people live, work, and interact with one another.

Language Time Travel: The Origin of "Dem-"

The root "dem-" comes from the Greek word *demos*, which means "people." In ancient Greece, the concept of *demos* was central to the idea of governance, particularly in democratic systems where citizens had a voice in how they were governed. Over time, this root expanded to encompass the study of populations (demographics), the spread of diseases among populations (epidemic and pandemic), and systems of government where the power lies with the people (democracy).

Story: The Power of Democracy

Maria was passionate about community involvement and believed in the power of democracy. After years of advocating for changes in her town, she finally saw her efforts pay off when she was elected to the town council. Her work focused on improving public health and education, believing that every person in the community deserved equal opportunities.

One of her most notable achievements was a public health initiative aimed at preventing the spread of disease, especially after a flu epidemic had impacted many families. Maria worked to create better healthcare facilities and improve awareness. As the years passed, her efforts helped the town become stronger and more united, a true reflection of the power of democracy where the people's voices led to meaningful change.

ROOT: "CRYPT-" (MEANING: "HIDDEN")

The root "crypt-" comes from the Greek word *kryptos*, meaning "hidden" or "secret." This root is used in words that refer to things that are concealed, secret, or difficult to understand. Many words derived from "crypt-" involve the idea of encoding, secrecy, or things that are not immediately visible or accessible.

Vocabulary:
1. **Cryptic**: Having a hidden meaning or something that is mysterious or puzzling.
    - *Example*: The message he left was cryptic, and no one could figure out what it meant.
2. **Cryptography**: The art of writing or solving codes, especially for securing communication and information.
    - *Example*: Modern cryptography is used to secure online transactions and protect sensitive data.
3. **Encrypt**: To convert information into a code to prevent unauthorized access, making it hidden from view.
    - *Example*: The files were encrypted to ensure that only authorized personnel could access them.
4. **Crypt**: An underground room or vault, often found in churches, used for burial or storage; also can refer to

anything that is hidden or secret.
- *Example*: The ancient crypt beneath the church was the final resting place of many notable figures.

Word Duel: Encrypt vs. Cryptic

Question: What's the difference between encrypt and cryptic?
- **Encrypt** refers to the process of converting information into a code to hide its meaning or to protect it from unauthorized access.
- **Cryptic** refers to something that is mysterious, puzzling, or has a hidden meaning, often requiring interpretation to understand.

Semantic Scale: From Hidden to Secured

This scale connects terms related to hiding or concealing information, from the mysterious to the secured:

1. **Cryptic** – Referring to something that is mysterious or has a hidden meaning, often requiring effort to decode.

Example: Her cryptic response left everyone wondering what she truly meant.

2. **Cryptography** – The science of securing communication and data by encoding information, making it unreadable without a key.

Example: The website uses advanced cryptography to protect users' personal information.

3. **Encrypt** – To encode information in such a way that only authorized users can access it, ensuring privacy and security.

Example: Before sending the sensitive email, they encrypted the contents to prevent leaks.

4. **Crypt** – An underground vault or room, often used for burials, or any hidden space or place.

Example: The explorers found an ancient crypt containing priceless artifacts.

Language Time Travel: The Origin of "Crypt-"

The root "crypt-" comes from the Greek word *kryptos*, which means "hidden" or "secret." Ancient civilizations used crypts as hidden burial chambers or secretive vaults, often associated with secrecy or sanctity. Over time, the idea of "hidden" expanded to encompass not just physical spaces, but also the concepts of encrypted messages and codes that protect sensitive information. The development of cryptography in the modern world is a natural extension of this root, as it focuses on keeping information secret from unauthorized access.

Story: The Mystery of the Hidden Code

Elena was a young cryptographer working for a top-secret government agency. One day, she was tasked with decrypting a series of messages intercepted from an unknown source. The messages were cryptic, filled with symbols and codes that seemed impossible to crack.

As she analyzed the data, Elena used her knowledge of cryptography to slowly break down the encryption. It took days of careful work, but finally, the hidden meaning behind the messages was revealed. They contained vital information about a potential security threat, which Elena reported immediately.

Her work had ensured that the hidden threats were uncovered, protecting many people from danger. It was a reminder that sometimes, the most important information is the hardest to find, hidden in plain sight, and it takes skill and persistence to uncover it.

ROOT: "CRE-" (MEANING: "CREATE" OR "GROW")

The root "cre-" comes from the Latin verb *creare*, meaning "to create" or "to grow." This root appears in words that are associated with making, producing, or bringing something into existence, as well as words related to growth or development.

Vocabulary:
1. **Create**: To bring something into existence, to produce or make something new.
    - *Example*: The artist will create a masterpiece for the gallery's new exhibit.
2. **Concrete**: A building material made from a mixture of cement, water, and aggregates, or something that is real, tangible, and solid.
    - *Example*: The workers poured concrete to form the foundation of the new building.
3. **Increase**: To make something larger, greater, or more in amount, degree, or size.
    - *Example*: The company plans to increase its production to meet the growing demand.
4. **Recreation**: Activities done for enjoyment, refreshment, or relaxation, often involving some form of creation or recreation of energy.
    - *Example*: After a long workweek, hiking in the

mountains was her favorite form of recreation.

Word Duel: Increase vs. Create

Question: What's the difference between increase and create?

- **Increase** refers to making something larger or more in quantity, size, or degree, often through gradual growth or addition.
- **Create** refers to bringing something entirely new into existence, making something that didn't exist before.

From Growth to Creation

These terms connect terms related to the idea of making or growing something, from gradual development to complete creation:

1. **Recreation** – Activities that renew or refresh, often related to play, hobbies, or enjoyment, which can lead to personal growth.

   Example: The community park offered a variety of recreational activities for people of all ages.

2. **Increase** – The act of growing or expanding in size, number, or degree.

   Example: The population of the city increased rapidly over the past decade.

3. **Concrete** – Something that is solid, tangible, and real, often referring to something that has been created and set in a permanent form.

   Example: The construction of the new school building is now made of concrete to ensure durability.

4. **Create** – To bring something into existence, often involving innovation, imagination, or effort to make something new.

   Example: The scientist will create a new formula to address the environmental crisis.

Language Time Travel: The Origin of "Cre-"

The root "cre-" comes from the Latin verb *creare*, meaning "to create" or "to grow." The idea of creation was central to many ancient cultures, both in the context of bringing things into being (like creating art or inventions) and in terms of growth, like plants or life. Over time, words related to *creare* evolved to describe not only the act of making but also the process of increasing or developing something. This root has influenced terms from basic creation to complex constructions and expansions in both literal and figurative senses.

The Growth of a Dream

Sophia had always dreamed of creating her own café. After years of working in the food industry, she finally saved enough money to open her own place. It wasn't easy, but with hard work and determination, she began to create a warm, inviting atmosphere that drew in customers.

As her business grew, Sophia focused on increasing her menu offerings, ensuring she provided new and exciting options for her regulars. She loved the recreation of energy that her café brought to the community, a space where people gathered to relax and share good food.

Years later, her café became a staple in the neighborhood, a testament to how creation, combined with growth and innovation, could turn a dream into something concrete and lasting.

ROOT: "COR-" (MEANING: "HEART")

The root "cor-" comes from the Latin word *cor*, meaning "heart." This root appears in words that refer to the literal or figurative heart, including concepts of emotion, central importance, and life force.

Vocabulary:
1. **Core**: The central, most important part of something; also, the innermost part of an object or idea.
    - *Example*: The core of the issue was a misunderstanding that could have been easily resolved with better communication.
2. **Courage**: The ability to face fear, danger, or difficulty with bravery; the mental strength to persevere.
    - *Example*: It took a lot of courage for her to speak out against the unfair treatment she witnessed.
3. **Discord**: Disagreement or conflict, especially a lack of harmony or unity.
    - *Example*: The meeting was filled with discord as the team couldn't agree on how to move forward with the project.
4. **Cardiologist**: A doctor who specializes in diagnosing and treating heart-related conditions.
    - *Example*: After experiencing chest pains, he visited a cardiologist for a thorough check-up.

Word Duel: Courage vs. Discord
Question: What's the difference between courage and discord?
- **Courage** refers to the mental or emotional strength to face challenges, fear, or adversity.
- **Discord** refers to a lack of harmony or agreement, often resulting in conflict or disagreement.

From Heartfelt to Heart-Related
These terms are related to the heart, from emotional strength to physical health:

1. **Courage** – The bravery or strength to act despite fear or difficulty, often from the "heart" in a metaphorical sense.

   Example: Her courage inspired the team to take risks and achieve their goals.

2. **Core** – The central, most important part of something, often referring to the essence of an idea or object.

   Example: The core values of the company include integrity and teamwork.

3. **Cardiologist** – A medical professional who specializes in heart health and diseases.

   Example: The cardiologist recommended lifestyle changes to prevent heart disease.

4. **Discord** – Disagreement or conflict, often linked to emotional or relational tension.

   Example: The discord between the two friends led to a long period of silence.

Language Time Travel: The Origin of "Cor-"
The root "cor-" comes from the Latin word *cor*, meaning "heart." In ancient times, the heart was seen as the seat of emotions, thoughts, and even courage. Over time, this symbolism of the heart expanded to words that reflect central importance (like *core*) or emotions (like *courage*). The development of medical terminology also brought about words like *cardiologist*, directly referring to the physical heart,

underscoring its vital role in human health.

The Heart of a Leader

Ana was known for her courage, always standing up for what she believed in and leading with her heart. When a major disagreement arose between the members of her organization, it created a lot of discord. Rather than letting it divide the group, Ana stepped in and sought to understand everyone's perspectives.

At the core of her leadership was empathy, as she encouraged everyone to communicate openly and work together toward a common goal. Over time, her actions brought the team back together, and they found a renewed sense of unity. Ana's ability to lead with courage and heart turned a difficult situation into an opportunity for growth and collaboration.

ROOT: "CLIN-" (MEANING: "LEAN" OR "SLOPE")

The root "clin-" comes from the Greek word *klinein*, meaning "to lean" or "to slope." It appears in words that refer to leaning, tilting, or sloping, as well as in terms related to medical care and practice, given its association with positions or shifts.

Vocabulary:
1. **Incline**: To lean or bend in a particular direction; also, a slope or a tendency toward something.
   - *Example*: The road began to incline as we approached the top of the hill.
2. **Decline**: To decrease or become lower in value, quality, or condition; also, to lean or slope downward.
   - *Example*: The patient's health began to decline after the surgery, requiring further attention.
3. **Clinic**: A facility where patients receive medical treatment, often specialized care or consultation.
   - *Example*: She went to the clinic for a check-up to ensure her health was on track.
4. **Clinician**: A healthcare professional who works directly with patients, such as a doctor, nurse, or therapist.
   - *Example*: The clinician recommended that I rest and drink plenty of fluids to recover from the flu.

Word Duel: Incline vs. Decline

Question: What's the difference between incline and decline?
- **Incline** refers to something leaning or sloping upwards, or a tendency or preference toward something.
- **Decline** refers to something leaning or sloping downwards, or a decrease in quantity, quality, or health.

Language Time Travel: The Origin of "Clin-"

The root "clin-" comes from the Greek *klinein*, meaning "to lean" or "to slope." Ancient Greek used this root to describe physical positions, such as a bed or reclining chair, and it evolved into words like *incline* and *decline* to describe slopes or shifts. Over time, this root also became associated with medical settings, such as *clinic* and *clinician*, due to the idea of patients reclining during treatment or examination.

Brief Storyline: A Shift in Health

Maria had always led a healthy, active lifestyle, but recently, she noticed her energy levels began to decline. Concerned, she visited her local clinic, where a clinician carefully examined her and ran several tests.

The clinician explained that while her health had declined due to stress and overwork, there was hope for improvement. With a plan in place to regain her strength, Maria made the necessary changes, including more rest and balanced nutrition.

Over time, she noticed an improvement in her health, and she gradually began to incline toward her old, active self. The experience taught her the importance of paying attention to her well-being and seeking care when needed.

ROOT: "CALOR-" (MEANING: "HEAT")

The root "calor-" comes from the Latin word *calor*, meaning "heat." It is found in words related to warmth, energy, or heat measurement, particularly in the context of food, energy, or temperature.

Vocabulary:
1. **Calorific**: Relating to or producing heat, especially in reference to the energy value of food.
   - *Example*: Foods that are high in fat are often considered calorific because they provide a large amount of energy.
2. **Calorie**: A unit of measurement for energy, commonly used to describe the energy content of foods.
   - *Example*: The salad contains fewer calories than a cheeseburger, making it a healthier option.
3. **Calorimeter**: An instrument used to measure the amount of heat involved in a chemical reaction or physical process.
   - *Example*: Scientists used a calorimeter to determine how much heat was released during the combustion of the fuel.

Word Duel: Calorie vs. Calorific
Question: What's the difference between calorie and calorific?

- **Calorie** refers to the unit of energy used to measure the energy content of food or the energy required for physical activity.
- **Calorific** describes something that produces or contains heat, especially when referring to the energy content of food.

From Heat Measurement to Energy
This list connects terms related to heat, from measuring it to understanding its energy content:

1. **Calorimeter** – A tool used to measure heat, especially during chemical reactions.

   Example: The calorimeter showed a significant increase in temperature after the reaction occurred.

2. **Calorie** – A unit of energy, often used to measure the energy content of food.

   Example: She kept track of her daily calorie intake to maintain a healthy diet.

3. **Calorific** – Describing something that produces or contains heat, particularly regarding the energy value of food.

   Example: The calorific value of a banana is lower than that of a chocolate bar.

Language Time Travel: The Origin of "Calor-"
The root "calor-" comes from the Latin *calor*, which means "heat." In ancient times, the concept of heat was central to understanding physical processes and food energy. As scientific understanding grew, particularly in nutrition and physics, the root "calor-" became associated with measuring energy, especially the energy in food. The terms *calorie* and *calorimeter* reflect this growing need to quantify and control heat and energy for practical and scientific purposes.

The Power of Heat
Lily, a nutritionist, was helping her client, Jake, understand the importance of calorific values in his diet. Jake

was trying to lose weight and had been counting calories, but he wasn't aware that not all calories are equal. Lily explained how different foods provide varying amounts of energy, and that understanding the calorific content of what he ate would help him make better choices.

To help demonstrate how food provided energy, Lily used a calorimeter to measure the energy released when a sample of food was burned. Jake was amazed at how heat could be used to measure the energy in food, and this newfound understanding motivated him to stick to a healthier diet, focusing not just on calories, but on the quality of the energy he was consuming.

ROOT: "BREV-" (MEANING: "SHORT")

The root "brev-" comes from the Latin word *brevis*, meaning "short." It appears in words related to being concise, brief, or short in duration.

Vocabulary:
1. **Abbreviate**: To shorten a word, phrase, or text by removing letters or using only the initial letters of words.
   - *Example*: The word "television" is often abbreviated to "TV."
2. **Brevity**: The quality of being brief or concise, particularly in speech or writing.
   - *Example*: The brevity of her speech impressed the audience, as she got straight to the point.
3. **Breviloquent**: Speaking briefly or concisely, often used in a formal context.
   - *Example*: His breviloquent style made him an excellent spokesperson for the company.
4. **Brief**: Short in duration, time, or length; also a written summary or statement.
   - *Example*: The meeting was brief, lasting only 20 minutes, but it covered all the important points.

Word Duel: Brief vs. Abbreviate
Question: What's the difference between brief and abbreviate?

- **Brief** refers to something that is short in duration, time, or length, or to a concise summary.
- **Abbreviate** refers to shortening a word or phrase by omitting parts of it, such as using "Dr." instead of "Doctor."

Semantic Scale: From Short Duration to Conciseness

This scale connects terms related to the idea of being short or concise, from time to language:

1. **Brief** – Something short in duration or length; also, a concise summary.

    Example: Her brief visit to the city was a whirlwind tour of the most famous landmarks.

2. **Brevity** – The quality of being brief and concise, especially in speech or writing.

    Example: The brevity of the statement made it all the more impactful.

3. **Abbreviate** – To shorten a word or phrase, usually by removing letters or using initials.

    Example: I had to abbreviate my essay to fit within the word limit.

4. **Breviloquent** – Speaking in a brief and concise manner.

    Example: The breviloquent professor delivered his lecture in just 30 minutes, covering everything we needed to know.

Language Time Travel: The Origin of "Brev-"

The root "brev-" comes from the Latin word *brevis*, meaning "short." In ancient times, brevity was valued in communication, especially in speeches and writings. The term *brevitas* (brevity) was used by Roman writers like Cicero to describe the art of being succinct while still conveying the necessary information. Over time, this root evolved into various terms such as *abbreviate, brevity*, and *brief*, all centered on the idea of conciseness.

The Power of Brevity

John, a speechwriter, was tasked with helping a

politician deliver a powerful message in just a few minutes. Understanding that brevity was key, he carefully crafted the speech, cutting out unnecessary words and focusing on the most impactful points. On the day of the event, the politician delivered the speech flawlessly, impressing the audience with its clarity and precision.

John knew that sometimes less is more, and his ability to use brevity effectively made all the difference in getting the message across. The politician's brief but powerful speech was remembered long after the event, proving that being concise can be far more impactful than saying too much.